To Rusty,

The Yankee Princess

The old tunes never fade
and the Bronx Zoo will
forever be a favorite...

Jennie Paul
" The Yankee Princess "
2011

The Yankee Princess

Why Dad and I Were In a
League of Our Own

Jennie Paul
with Jody Lynn Smith

The Silloway Press

Columbia, MD

The Yankee Princess:
Why Dad and I Were in a League of Our Own
© 2011 Jennie Paul. All rights reserved
Published by The Silloway Press
Columbia, MD

"Tricia Hears it From the Fans" — Copyright NYP Holdings, Inc. Reprinted with Permission.

"Ziggy" cartoon — Ziggy © 1980 Ziggy & Friends, Inc. Used courtesy of Tom Wilson and Tom Wilson II. Universal Uclick. All rights reserved.

"'Catfish' hooked for $3.75 million" — Used with permission of *The Tampa Tribune.*

Gabe Paul's diaries, other photos and documents from the collection of Jennie Paul.

Cover design by Mudpuddle Creations.
www.MudpuddleCreations.com

ISBN-13: 978-0-9826293-3-8
ISBN-10: 0-9826293-3-8
LCCN: 2010937415

Printed in the United States of America

The Silloway Press
www.SillowayPress.com
Email: YP@SillowayPress.com

In memory of my mentors,

Shirley Povich of *The Washington Post*,

Noted sports writer Mark Asher,

and

Si Burick, sports editor of the *Dayton Daily News*

Matthew and McKenzie Gardner

For Matthew and McKenzie

You are your grandfather's legacy and my inspiration
Dream
Live your dreams
Have passion
Be willing to take the risk
Tell the truth
Make your word your bond
And remember…
I love you no matter what.

Contents

Foreword

The best books about sports are written by the players them-selves because they provide inside information that the reader cannot pick up by reading a newspaper or a magazine. I was an insider who had a front row seat watching the New York Yan-kees during their Bronx Zoo years. I wrote books with Sparky Lyle, Billy Martin, Graig Nettles, and Ron Guidry. I heard all the stories — or at least I thought I had.

It turns out there was a hidden "player" involved with all the principle figures on the Yankees, a woman who was privy to the private boxed world of owner George Steinbrenner, general man-ager and president Gabe Paul, and the star players such as Reggie Jackson and Thurman Munson. Behind the curtains, she was also engaged in a secret affair with Yankee manager Billy Martin. She worked as a sports reporter, but the reason she had such complete access was that she was Gabe Paul's daughter, Jennie.

In her twenties Jennie Paul attempted to forge a career in sports journalism while at the same time not upsetting the Yankee top brass and getting her father in trouble with her reports. Considering that George Steinbrenner and her father Gabe Paul both owned the Yankees, along with a number of other behind-the-scenes characters, Jennie had an extremely difficult if not impossible task. Several times, Jennie was in a position to enhance her TV career with important late-breaking stories about the Yankees only to have her father demonstrate that his allegiance to the Yankees was far more important than his loyalty to his daughter.

It made her a little meshuganah. Desperate for her father's love — what she calls the daddy hole — she reached out to powerful, domineering men to fill the void. As she put it, they were unhealthy choices but she could not help herself. One of those choices was her daddy's bad boy manager, Billy Martin. Jennie knew Martin to be an alcoholic and a serial philanderer with a national reputation, but Billy, who was a practiced seducer, showered her with kindness, and she was smitten. They carried on a relationship off and on until Billy died on Christmas day of 1990.

This book is fascinating in the same way people love watching train wrecks. You know you should not be watching, but you cannot take your eyes off what is happening to Jennie. You wish she would make better decisions, but when she talks about why she does what she does, it becomes unmistakably clear that she really had no alternative. Why couldn't Gabe Paul, her dad, have paid more attention to his daughter's wants and needs? It's a story that I'm certain plays itself out over and over in families all over America. Yankee fans will learn a lot, and so will fathers and daughters. *Yankee Princess* reads a lot like Oprah meets George Steinbrenner. Who can resist?

Peter Golenbock
St. Petersburg, Florida
December 2009

Acknowledgments

I was sitting on my couch in Annapolis, MD one hot summer day when the voice on the other end of the phone said, "Hi, I am Burton Rocks. You need to finish your book." After reading Mark Herrmann's full-page article in New York's *Newsday* titled "She's Tooting the Horn for Gabe," *New York Times* bestselling author Burton was the one to cheer me on and make me realize there was a lot to be told. He encouraged me to continue when I was discouraged and overwhelmed. Burton, I appreciate you and your kindness.

To sports writer Eric Butterman, I thank you for helping with certain difficult emotional parts of the book. My favorite line you helped with is that "A father is just a phone call away, but that will now only be a one way call...Dad, I love you."

To Peter Golenbock, one of America's greatest sports authors, you took the time in a busy schedule to read *The Yankee Princess* and offer your opinion. You promised to tell the truth. You not only told me it was fantastic but made valuable suggestions and wrote the Foreword. I appreciate your input, time, honesty and strength of character.

To Dave Anderson, the Pulitzer Prize-winning *New York Times* sports writer who agreed to do the same, and to Mark Herrmann from *Newsday,* thank you. I am flattered.

To my beautiful children Matthew and McKenzie, you can now read about what was behind some of my frustrations and what an impact a family member can have on you for your whole life. I am sure you will continue building your lives with your own inner convictions as you grow knowing Dad and I loved and will continue to love you despite our frailties.

To my Mom, the beautiful beauty queen, who at the writing of this book is still living, although not like you and Dad did. God bless you always. You are a free spirit. I know you held it in, but I appreciate that spirit. I love you, Mama. Don't worry that I took that spirit and rightly or wrongly ran with it, which was enough for both of us.

To Dad's dear New York Yankees secretary, Pearl Davis. Thank you for your encouragement, additions to the book, and advice to get the book out sooner rather than later in honor of my father. You are beautiful, Pearl. Dad loved you. Thanks for not underestimating The Yankee Princess.

All of Dad's secretaries had the utmost respect for him. Thank you, though, to Barbara Lessman who so lovingly honored his presence in Cleveland when he left the Yankees after winning the World Series. That was a fragile time and you did a great job making Dad feel welcome. I admire your loyalty working for the Indicans' top brass your whole career.

Every once in a while when you do not know what to expect, something very nice happens. My publisher, Peg Silloway, was the backbone in this process. Your input, advice, and experience were essential factors in actually releasing the story that was so hard for me to write. You took much of the anxiety off my shoulders, and your forthright and honest comments were invaluable. Your humor was much appreciated. Thank you for all that you did, Peg, to improve this father-daughter manuscript.

Finally, to my baby brother Henry Lee who in his own right struggled with similar things as I did. You said Dad would be proud. You are not always what you do but who you are. Hen, you are one of the kindest and gentlest souls I have ever known. You are a true Renaissance man. Your encouragement means the world to me. I love you.

Introduction

I handed the clerk at the small Maryland post office one of those annoying yellow slips, wondering what was waiting for me. I didn't remember ordering anything from my favorite mail order places. I was in a failing marriage, raising two kids alone. Sometimes, I did forget things. My brothers were forever saying, "Jennie, don't you remember?" to which I would always reply with a slightly bewildered, "I guess not." But the stresses of a pending divorce did not make me forget my past. I was quite clear on what happened to me in my life. Sometimes I remembered more than I wanted to.

As the woman behind the counter returned with the box, I saw the return address and understood. I wondered if she could even begin to fathom how I felt when she said, "Here you go, Miss." I was not being rude for not saying, "Thank you." All I could muster was, "My dad is inside here."

I turned quickly so no one could see the tears as I carried him out to my car. I drove around aimlessly for a long time with Dad's ashes before I could get the courage to open that box. To my surprise, I found a note revealing that in addition to his ashes, Dad had willed his personal files and diary to me. A sudden realization swept over me; Dad had left everything that remained of him, all that he had — his legacy — to me. In that moment I flashed back to my life as the only daughter of the owner of four major league baseball teams, and wondered if now I would finally understand what had happened to us.

Baseball has always seemed to be for fathers and sons. "Field of Dreams" ends with Kevin Costner asking that tear drenched question: "Dad…wanna have a catch?" Makes us weep every time, even the most unfeeling of the lot. But that is just a made-for-Hollywood story. And the idea that baseball is just between boys and their dads? Also a fairy tale. I know because I was once a princess, or, as I like to say bittersweetly, a Yankee Princess.

My dad, Gabe Paul, was president of the New York Yankees when they were in desperate need of a champion. The Mantles and Marises had long since left the city that never sleeps, and the Bronx Bombers had sunk into a seemingly endless losing streak. It seemed that maybe "Damn Yankees" was just a Broadway show after all. But then my father brought the blasphemy back to the team name by convincing shipbuilder and risk-taker George Steinbrenner III to join in the group that he was putting together to purchase the pinstriped hopefuls in 1973 (Steinbrenner actually wanted to own the Cleveland Indians and Detroit Tigers). It was Dad, in fact, who traded for ice-water-veined heroes like Jim "Catfish" Hunter, and who kept Steinbrenner, Reggie Jackson, and Billy Martin from strangling each other in front of season ticket-holders. I should know: I dated the last of that triumvirate, something which I think would have hurt my dad deeply if he had known.

Baseball is like the relationship I had with my father: a lot of standing around, but every once in a while something truly amazing happens which easily makes up for the price of admission. Dad and I connected through baseball — as much as he could connect, anyway — leading me into a life of sportscasting, writing for the *Sporting News*, and chasing my father's dream even if it wasn't my own. Despite this, I never got what I really wanted and needed from him. While Dad was in newspapers, books, mini-series and talked about in sports bars across America, my life was spiraling out of control.

This bottomless hole led to an abusive marriage, a distrust of people, and never actually knowing who I was. My dad made baseball history with the relationships he formed with difficult people like George Steinbrenner, Howard Cosell, Billy Martin, Tommy Lasorda, Jackie Robinson, Frank Robinson and so many more, but he was unable to build a supportive relationship with his only daughter.

The ESPN mini-series, "The Bronx is Burning," told a small sliver of Dad's story, and to high ratings, I might add, but now I'm here to finish it. To tell the truth about Dad being much more than a "yes" man, about all that Steinbrenner was and wasn't, that Billy Martin was far more than just an angry, womanizing alcoholic, that Reggie Jackson wasn't just a verbose blundering moron, and to once and for all do away with the "Field of Dreams" myth that this game is just for fathers and sons. No, it's so much more than that. It's for everyone who believes that next season might just be The One. We all want to believe that.

I wondered if that final gesture from Dad of willing all his files to me was his way of telling me everything that he always wanted to say and could never explain. I knew there was a story there, and I knew I had much more; I felt as if my dad had finally reached out to me with open arms.

That meant it was time for his little Yankee Princess to wipe off the pine tar, dig into the box and summon the courage to see what I might muster for him. A homerun? Well, maybe, although I'll gladly settle for the equivalent of a triple. I don't think I could ever tell the complete story of my father's life or our relationship struggle. I knew about all the pain he caused me with his small slights and silence; Dad was a hero to many and an antagonist to me. As I made my way through his story, I understood how others hurt him and more about what he endured during his years with the Yankees, Indians, Reds, and Colt .45s as others stole the credit for his achievements. And I realized that I had something that no one else had that would make my version of Gabe Paul's story unique — I WAS THERE.

Dad's weary body gave out in 1998, and though the obituaries said all the right things, when he died he was unheralded, unappreciated, and frankly, tired. Some say it was age, but like so many men of his generation who had trouble expressing their feelings, it might have been his heart which finally burst from keeping so much in.

This is our story as no other can tell it. I tried to be as accurate as possible with dates, times, and places, although if I missed something it is because there was so much to review and there is an enormous amount of information available to me. Time blurs some details, but the truth comes through.

Fathers and daughters, like owners and managers, managers and players, players and fans, and just about every pair of people, often misunderstand one another. Going through Dad's diary and notes, I was struck by the honesty and emotion he expressed privately. And I found that the one way I could respond now and express my feelings best was to write him letters — a sort of diary duet that you will find with each New York chapter.

A woman may go her whole life looking for her father, which is sad because usually he's just a phone call away. For me, there will be no more calls except for this one-way conversation sent with all my love.

I miss you, Dad.

1

From Bat Boy to Big Deal

Wid Matthews had seen the kid before, hanging around the ball-park that summer of 1920. Maybe it was the look on the 10-year-old's face that caught Wid's attention, himself a young southpaw in the minor leagues. There were always boys hanging on the fence, dreaming of glory on the diamond. But this one was different — he was focused, intent, and absolutely entranced by baseball.

Matthews invited the kid on to the field to be a batboy for the Rochester Red Wings of the International League, and set into motion a career that would bring triumph, disappointment, and a life-long love affair with the game. Over the years, that kid — Gabriel Howard Paul — would be called many things, but for me he would have only one name…Dad.

Gabe Paul's involvement in the organizational side of baseball took off later in the 1920's when Cincinnati Reds general manager and president Warren Giles lured Dad away from his early career as batboy, bullpen catcher, and beginning sports writer to become Giles' press secretary. Dad was just the fourth public relations man in major league baseball. Under Giles' wing Gabe thrived learning front office tactics and fundamentally sound operations as the Cincinnati Reds earned their way to a pennant in 1940. When Warren Giles accepted the position of National League President in 1951, Dad succeeded him to take the top position with the Reds.

Cincinnati Reds celebrate winning the 1940 National League pennant
Gabe Paul in suit at center

With that step up, Dad became the youngest major league team president and general manager in baseball history. It was the first of many important milestones in his life.

In 1956, my Dad won the highly coveted award as the *Sporting News* Baseball Executive of the Year for his business acumen in running the Cincinnati team, and signing players like Rookie of the Year Frank Robinson, along with Gus Bell, Wally Post, Ted Kluszewski, and Ed Bailey. Together, these sluggers whacked 221 homers that season. The Cincinnati Reds finished third in the National League, and they were a pennant contender.

Gabe Paul knew how to run a team and draw fans into the park. In one public relations coup, Dad ensured that the National League all-star team was almost entirely a Reds team, by using the power of suggestion and a consistent message in the local newspapers. For two straight weeks before the all-star team selection, Dad advertised a picture of the ballot with checkmarks next to the names of every Reds starting player. On voting day, many fans that came to the game marked their ballots with the same players as shown in the newspaper ad. Eight Reds and one "outsider," Stan Musial, were voted onto the all-star team. The commissioner intervened and rebalanced the team before the game, but all of Cincinnati rejoiced anyway.

Gabe understood the value of a strong farm team system to groom promising young players and produce future baseball superstars. He brought such famous names as Curt Flood, Pete Rose, Johnny Bench, Vada Pinson, Tommy Harper, and Jim Maloney up from farm teams to enrich baseball.

In 1960, Cincinnati Reds owner Powell Crosley was interested in following the lead of the Giants and Dodgers who had recently left New York City for new home fields in San Francisco and Los Angeles. Crosley weighed the benefits of leaving Ohio, and my dad made a strong case for keeping the team in the city he loved.

After 24 years with the Reds and raising a family of five children, all of whom were born in Cincinnati, Dad was ready for more responsibility and control. He approached Crosley, who was also a dear friend, about buying the majority stake in the Reds. Word gets around quickly in major league baseball, particularly when it concerns the possibility of a team for sale. Powell Crosley was not ready to sell the team, but he vowed to support Dad in keeping the Reds where they were.

Dad's diary reflects his disappointment when Crosley tried to have it both ways:

"I convinced Powell to sign a statement pledging that the club would never leave Cincinnati in his lifetime. When he asked the league for permission to play 21 games in New York, I wanted to move out."

Through the relationship with his mentor Warren Giles, who was still National League President, Gabe discovered that the National League had succumbed to the pressure to grant an expansion team franchise to Houston. Four rich and powerful Texans — George Kirksey, Craig Cullinan, R.E. "Bob" Smith, and Judge Roy Hofheinz, the former mayor of Houston — had threatened to begin their own new Continental Circuit if the league did not give them a home team. The owners of the Colt .45s (which would ultimately become the Houston Astros) had made several inquiries and attempts to lure Dad away from Cincinnati. He had always declined, but now in a moment of frustration, he left Cincinnati abruptly taking our whole family with him.

Gabe and Mary Frances Paul

I believe that is when our father-daughter problems truly began, and somehow these problems grew with each move and each of the teams he owned, especially the New York Yankees.

Dad found he liked the style of the Texan expansion team founders. He signed a three-year contract lured by the promise of power and control. Kirksey, a long-time friend of Gabe's, helped negotiate the deal. Dad remarked at the press conference, "It was done in a day to keep me from changing my mind."

Dad's acceptance of the position was big news. The fact that Dad was married to a former Miss Florida Orange Queen and aspiring actress who had given up her dream to support her husband and raise a family, endeared us and him to the Colt .45s.

The local papers featured family photographs almost as often as articles on the progress of the ballpark, which would become the Houston Astrodome.

If it is true that a picture is worth a thousand words, the hundreds of newspaper clippings on Dad's work with the start-up team and our family explain a lot about the man I called "Dad."

Everything was big in Houston, and Dad knew how to work it to his advantage. the *Sporting News*, also known as "the Bible of sports reporting," covered it all. Dad was front-page news and he was one of their own, a former reporter who had made it big. He said, "The Houston owners mean business and their program down there is one of the most proficient I have ever known. It is all calculated to get as many good players as possible."

Dad was given the freedom to make decisions and spend money. He had found the ideal place to do what he always wanted — to build a winning team. The challenge invigorated him, and the glint in his eye and Mom's, according to comments found in clippings contained in his diary, made them seem ten years younger. Gabe brought Warren Giles' son Bill, who would later own the Philadelphia Phillies, with him and together they went to work preparing for a 1962 debut in Texas.

But the trouble started quickly as Judge Roy Hofheinz realized that Dad was upstaging his local celebrity status. The judge had lots of experience in PR and very little in baseball. According to Dad' diary, Hofheinz's large expenditures for huge Texas-style promotional events prompted Dad to say to Bill Giles, "This place is beginning to look like a used car lot!"

Hofheinz in turn challenged Dad on seemingly minor operational business decisions that I believe Dad would have seen as a fight for control and a disrespecting of baseball ritual. One example was the judge's insistence that the name of each player be announced each time he went up to bat. Tradition called for the names to be announced only the first time at bat. Gabe argued that program sales would be hurt. "The heck with program sales," thundered Hofheinz. "We announce them every time at bat."

It was an odd fight considering that the Astrodome, a "revolutionary domed stadium" with a demountable glass roof, wasn't even built yet and the team, which Gabe was still building, had yet to play a game. When the judge announced that fans would see their team play sooner than expected in a new temporary stadium, Gabe was upset at the waste of money and feared what it would do to his own plans for the team. Gabe felt the money could be better spent establishing a farm system. He fought for it and Craig Cullinan, one of the original four partners, strongly supported him. Hofheinz acquiesced — for a short period — while Gabe began to mount one of the largest recruitment efforts in major league baseball at that time.

Dad told reporters, "We will be a master scouting system second to none in the majors. It's going to cost money, lots of it, but our people are willing to pay to see the system through. We've divided the nation into 17 areas with a top scout to be named for each. There will be sub-scouts and bird dogs until we have approximately 500 men combing the fields for prospects for our club. In addition, we have lined up international representatives for the Mexican, Caribbean, and Canadian areas."

In Houston the ball was rolling, but something was amiss. Soon Cullinan, the partner with whom Dad had the greatest affinity outside his long-term friend Kirksey, was forced out of the group. My father started to question his ability to run and win with the team under these conditions and with a correspondingly fast-dwindling budget; he let it be known that he regretted his decision to leave Ohio.

In photos we looked like the perfect made-for-TV family of the day, but something very painful had happened in Texas. Although Gabe refused to talk about it, a number of reporters suggested that Dad experienced prejudice and exclusion because he was Jewish. Knowing Dad the way I did, I am sure social prejudice hurt him. My brothers and I were raised Episcopal, an agreement Mom and Dad made before they married. Dad did not fear discrimination; he just chose to keep his faith private.

Warren, Jennie, Michael, Gabe Jr., Gabe, Henry, and Mary Frances Paul

For the most part, my dad kept his fears about prejudice regarding his religion and the business of baseball separate. Still, I am certain Dad would not walk away from a job because of religion. But he would absolutely walk away from a hotel to take a stand for players on his team denied access due to their skin color. If his players were not welcome, then the team executive did not patronize the business. That is how it was for Dad.

Shortly after opening day in 1961, my dad resigned from the Houston organization to take over as general manager for the Cleveland Indians, ousting Frank "Trader" Lane, a peer and rival with whom Dad had often traded jibes when he ran the Reds. Dad's contract with Cleveland provided him with an 11 percent ownership stake in the team. "We belong in Ohio," he told the family.

Dad's diary includes remarks to the press from Bobby Bragan, a former Pirates and Indians manager, who coached the Dodgers and was the Houston scouting director when Dad was there. He speculated, "It is my guess, and it's strictly that, the reason Gabe left Houston was over a difference of opinion with Mr. Big of the Houston Sports Association." Mr. Big, of course, was Roy Hofheinz. This same Mr. Big was quoted as saying, "I don't know a damn thing about baseball, and I don't intend to interfere. What's the need of hiring a top horse if you're going to have to try and drag the wagon yourself?" This was the same man who touted his own latest PR move (after Dad left) aimed at boosting ticket sales. His idea placed scantily clad servers in a single restaurant on the visitors' side of the ballpark concessions. Small wonder he and Gabe Paul did not see eye to eye.

Back in Cleveland, Dad was firmly entrenched in a place and with a group of men he understood. He started making things happen for his new home team by getting the business on track and attracting fans with a ball club worthy of its fans and their hometown. In 1961, the Indians finished the regular season in fifth place with 78 wins and 83 losses, trailing the pennant-winning Yankees by more than 30 games. That same year the Cincinnati Reds, the team Dad had been with for 24 years before his short stint in Houston, won the National League pennant.

In the 1961 World Series, Dad's first team, the Reds, would face the Yankees, his future team. Dad's current team, the Cleveland Indians, would watch from home.

The Reds' Powell Crosley had died six months after Dad left Cincinnati for Houston. By the time Dad returned to Ohio with the Indians, Powell Crosley Jr. had sold the team to Bill DeWitt. Joe Rippe, who was the banker for that deal, told me later he believed that if Dad had not left Cincinnati in 1960 our family would own the Reds today. According to what Joe told me and my brother Henry, the sale of the Reds had some irregularities sufficient to warrant the attention of the Ohio Attorney General, and an investigation ensued. The sale could have been overturned at that time and Joe and a number of other buyers saw it as an opportunity to bring a man who knew more about the Reds than anyone home to lead them. They would try to buy the Reds if Dad would be the general partner and president. But he felt there were political undertones that had infiltrated his beloved Reds, and Dad said "No." He chose to stick to the handshake deal he made with Bill Daley and Nate Dolan with the Indians. Dad would buy into the Cleveland Indians and not the Cincinnati Reds. His word was his bond.

If Dad had asked any of us in the family, we all would have told him to leave Cleveland and go back to Cincinnati. Dad did not ask. He walked away from the chance to own the Reds.

His commitment not to abandon the Indians after agreeing to be part of the new ownership group did have the positive effect of strengthening many of Dad's relationships in Cleveland.

Those relationships would later form the basis of a buying group that Dad assembled to buy the New York Yankees. Would the Yankees be where they are today if Dad had not eventually walked away from them, too? No one can say. What is for sure, though, is that Gabe Paul walked away from much of what he loved — personally and professionally — over the years. The Cincinnati Reds happened to come first.

Note to Gabe from Jackie Robinson

Dad's deal-making expertise helped remedy many of the front office blunders that had led to the Indians dropping from the number two position that they once held. Dad traded Jim Piersall for Dick Donovan, Gene Green and Jim Mahoney plus

$25,000 cash. He got home run slugging Chuck Essegian, Jerry Kindall, Pedro Ramos, Tito Francona, and pitching greats Sam McDowell and Luis Tiant. He said, "In this trading business of you win' em and you lose 'em, a lot of luck enters into it."

Dad also negotiated a complex three way deal to bring back Rocky Colavito, a fan-favorite, whom Frank Lane had traded away cheap. Frank's decision angered fans, and attendance dropped severely. Getting Rocky back cost the Indians too much young talent, Dad wrote, yet he knew he needed the ticket sales that Rocky would bring. But when Rocky did not perform as expected, the fans stopped coming again. It was a costly mistake and it haunted Dad. He did not like to make mistakes.

Gabe Paul with Lamar Hunt in Dallas

The Yankees would defeat the Cincinnati Reds in the 1961 World Series. They would also take the 1962 World Series championship the following year, besting the San Francisco Giants for back-to-back championships. After the 1962 season, Dad would fend off several interested buyers who wanted to move the Cleveland ball club out of town. Instead, he finalized a contract that would make him the principal owner of the Indians by 1963, ensuring that the team stayed put. Dad focused on his team, keeping his word and commitments.

Dad built relationships that helped to ensure that the Indians would stay in Cleveland despite strong interest by some of the directors to consider relocation offers in 1964 from Seattle, Oakland, and Dallas.

Dad, Vernon Stouffer, and several other directors made a strong pitch for the value of staying in Cleveland. Bill Daley, who seemed to care only about selling for the most money, advised the directors not to be swayed on emotional pressure incited by Cleveland newspapers which had much to lose if the Indians left Cleveland.

Despite a chance to make a large return on his investment in the Indians, Dad squashed each attempt to move the team. In 1965, Dad was offered the job as Commissioner of Baseball, but he turned it down for the same reason he rejected Rippe's appeal to leave the Indians. He had agreed to fight for his team and he wasn't leaving before the fight was won. For Dad, loyalty was more important than money. His goal was keeping the team in Cleveland with enough capital to build a winning ball club that could meet payroll without having to trade away star players like "Mudcat" Grant.

Dad felt that the secret to operating the Indians continuously and successfully — and keeping them in Cleveland — was old money. He appealed to Vernon Stouffer, of Stouffer's Foods and

Stouffer Hotels, to buy the team from his group. Dad agreed to continue running it for Vernon, who admittedly knew very little about baseball. Stouffer planned to invest $1,000,000 to rebuild the team, and by 1968, it looked like the deals that Dad was making could catapult the Indians out of their historic middle-of-the-pack standings to the first Indian pennant since 1954.

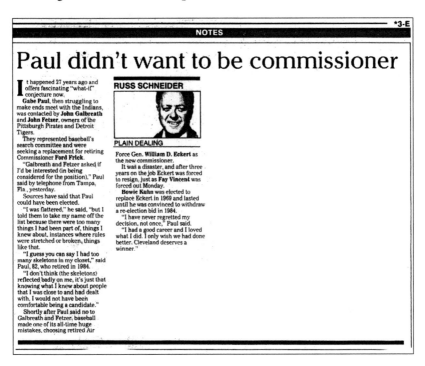

*3-E

NOTES

Paul didn't want to be commissioner

RUSS SCHNEIDER

PLAIN DEALING

It happened 27 years ago and offers fascinating "what-if" conjecture now.

Gabe Paul, then struggling to make ends meet with the Indians, was contacted by John Galbreath and John Fetzer, owners of the Pittsburgh Pirates and Detroit Tigers.

They represented baseball's search committee and were seeking a replacement for retiring Commissioner Ford Frick.

"Galbreath and Fetzer asked if I'd be interested (in being considered for the position)," Paul said by telephone from Tampa, Fla., yesterday.

Sources have said that Paul could have been elected.

"I was flattered," he said, "but I told them to take my name off the list because there were too many things I had been part of, things I knew about, instances where rules were stretched or broken, things like that.

"I guess you can say I had too many skeletons in my closet," said Paul, 82, who retired in 1984.

"I don't think (the skeletons) reflected badly on me, it's just that knowing what I knew about people that I was close to and had dealt with, I would not have been comfortable being a candidate."

Shortly after Paul said no to Galbreath and Fetzer, baseball made one of its all-time huge mistakes, choosing retired Air Force Gen. William D. Eckert as the new commissioner.

It was a disaster, and after three years on the job Eckert was forced to resign, just as Fay Vincent was forced out Monday.

Bowie Kuhn was elected to replace Eckert in 1969 and lasted until he was convinced to withdraw a re-election bid in 1984.

"I have never regretted my decision, not once," Paul said. "I had a good career and I loved what I did. I only wish we had done better. Cleveland deserves a winner."

It was not to be. In an unrelated deal, Vernon had exchanged a portion of his Stouffer's stock for stock in Litton Industries. When the share value of Litton Industries dropped 100 points, Vernon was almost broke, and the cash inflow that Gabe was counting on to run the team all but stopped. The farm system and scouting budgets also took a severe hit. The following season the Indians finished low, and Stouffer, who was drinking heavily, publicly blamed Gabe. Ticket sales dropped, and at Stouffer's insistence Dad gave up his general manager title to Alvin Dark, who had

Stouffer's ear and was more than willing to use that access to advance his own agenda.

My dad, who saw what Dark was doing, thought him utterly incompetent. He tried to tell Vernon; however, Vernon was stubborn in his support for Alvin. Dark made several disastrous trades. In less than a year, Vernon fired Alvin and Dad had his old job back. In a bizarre twist, Alvin later turned preacher and wrote Dad a letter apologizing for his backstabbing ways.

Stouffer was not a self-made man like Dad, having attended the Wharton School before returning to Ohio to work in the business his parents had created. But he cared about Cleveland, just like Dad. Vernon Stouffer's financial difficulties and very public alcohol abuse put Dad in a difficult position that tested his ability to maintain a working relationship with the principal owner who had openly disrespected him. Dad knew that Vernon was still a good man deep down even though Stouffer didn't always behave well.

After several years of trying to run the Indians on a shoestring with little or no money, it became clear that Vernon Stouffer could no longer keep the team. According to Dad's files, Stouffer was surprised that Clevelanders would not support the team by buying tickets "out of civic duty," and was willing to sell the Indians to an out-of-town buyer. Of course, Dad's first choice would be a buyer committed to keeping the team in Cleveland.

Leveraging his strong relationships in business and baseball, Dad tried to buy the team back from Vernon. The principal owners in this bid included himself, Francis "Steve" O'Neill, a trucking company owner, Al Rosen, the former ballplayer, and George Steinbrenner, a shipbuilding executive. Gabe was to be in charge when the deal went through. Since Vernon and George, who had owned the Cleveland Pipers basketball team, were both sports team owners, it seemed logical for Steinbrenner to take the lead on making the offer to Stouffer. Remaining in the background given his position and current state of his relationship with Stouffer served Dad well. The initial offer was for $5 million, and Gabe thought it was a good number. Dad knew Vernon needed the money.

Stouffer immediately refused it in an emotional decision based on an affront from long ago. Unknown to Gabe, Steinbrenner had once "borrowed" something valuable from Stouffer's son without asking. Steinbrenner had attempted to repair the damage first with Vernon's son and then with Stouffer himself, and upped his offer to $6,000,000. George balked, though, when Stouffer said he wanted $9 million.

File memo written by Gabe Paul

Dad distanced himself from the Steinbrenner offer and instead exercised his option to purchase an additional ten percent of Indians stock directly from Stouffer for $250,000. This gave the Indians operating cash while Vernon struggled with his need to sell the team. It also created a win-win situation for

Dad and the Indians. According to our family records, Gabe now owned twenty percent of the Indians (contrary to newspaper reports at the time that he owned much less.) With that done, Dad became the largest stockholder in the team next to Vernon. The negotiations and offers from several would-be suitors continued.

Publicly Dad said, "I am making the purchase as a show of faith in the club." Privately, my dad was taking care of himself, Mom, and our family in his way. Dad did not believe in giving handouts to his children. Dad made it with hard work, and he wanted his children to do the same. That message came across loud and clear at home, though of course we didn't appreciate the value of the lesson at that time.

Steinbrenner and Al Rosen eventually came up to Stouffer's asking amount, but it was too late. Vernon was already being courted for a shared franchise deal between Cleveland and the city of New Orleans. The American League would not approve the deal until a feasibility study was completed on this novel concept. Meanwhile, another bid was entered by Cleveland Cavaliers owner Nick Mileti and unnamed investors.

Dad purposely stayed out of the negotiations, having abandoned his potential role with George on the Indians' purchase. The Mileti group came up with the $9 million that Stouffer wanted, and the deal was done on July 31, 1972. The sale of the Indians rewarded Dad handsomely, even though it was ultimately restructured to include $6 million in debt assumption and capital with additional annual payments to Stouffer. Mileti vowed to do everything he could to keep the Indians in their hometown.

2
A Bite of the Big Apple

Once my dad committed to something, he did what he said he would do. That value gave him the big break that he needed to see his life's dream come true...for a little while anyway. Dad began to expand his network and net worth among those Cleveland Indian fans who, like him, felt that they were missing something in life that they so clearly deserved — a winning baseball team of their own. This shared sentiment got him a seat at Table 14 at the Pewter Mug near Public Square on more than one important occasion. This favorite, wood paneled restaurant was the unofficial meeting place of the City of Cleveland's power players, and Table 14 was reserved for the top movers and shakers — men like George Steinbrenner and Art Modell.

Dad and Modell had been friends for many years, but their relationship soured when they butted heads over the stadium lease. Modell had negotiated a contract for the Cleveland Municipal Stadium under which he paid the city a token $1 and took over all the operating and maintenance costs of that run-down facility where the Browns and Indians played. Dad had planned to get a better deal for the Indians, but Modell refused and kept the rent high for the Indians while keeping all the parking and concession income for himself. Time would prove that he needed that money because the stadium was in worse shape than anyone knew, but that did not matter to Gabe and his ball club.

By the summer of 1972, Dad was no longer a fan of Modell. He thought Modell was unprincipled and not very civic-minded, given the sorry financial state of the Indians and Dad's desire to keep the team in Cleveland. Dad would no longer sit at the same table as Art.

Serendipity was Dad's friend on a hot summer night in 1972 when he sat down at Table 14 next to George Steinbrenner, who this time was not with Art Modell, his frequent dinner companion. (Perhaps Dad was the "ultimate baseball survivor," just as Pete Franklin, the famous Cleveland sportscaster, had called him. Pete said Dad was intelligent, a great self-promoter, and a person who knew how to get next to people with money.) That night, when my dad joined Steinbrenner at Table 14, George was literally crying in his beer over the news he had just received from Vernon Stouffer: Nick Mileti and not George would be the new owner of the Indians.

Dad already knew that Vernon had chosen another buyer, but he had purposely not called George to tell him. Instead, he chose to listen, something that he did all his baseball life. It was dad's strength. Steinbrenner confided that he had lost face and his shot at his dream but he was not about to give up. Adopting an "I'll show him" posture, George told Gabe that he planned to try to buy the Detroit Tigers.

Gabe Paul was a master behind the scenes and had an ability to think on his feet. To Gabe, dinner at Table 14 that night was like winning both games in a doubleheader at a crucial point in the season. He offered George an out — the kind you like in baseball.

"Well Gabe," George said, "it looks like you and I are not going to run the Indians together. I would have taken care of you and Art. The stadium issue would not have been a problem anymore."

Dad didn't want to talk about Art. "I did alright, George."

"I want a team, Gabe. I'm going to get a team," said George.

"Hmm, well hopefully, we will be playing each other," Dad offered. (I wonder, was Dad predicting the future without knowing it?)

"What about the Indians facing me as the owner of Detroit?" George asked.

"Well, I don't know about Detroit," Dad replied.

"Gabe, I could do things for Detroit that I couldn't do here. If I were leading that team instead of…let's just say your Indians would be in big trouble. Nick paid too much, by the way."

George didn't know it, but Dad was considering the purchase of another team. With the members in his proposed limited liability partnership, Gabe had what he needed to meet the price Michael Burke (then President of the New York Yankees) thought CBS would take for the team. However, Dad feared that he would not have enough operating capital to run the team his way. Gabe's decision to make a bid for the New York Yankees was not about ownership alone. To own a team and not have the money to run it properly was not something he would consider. But George was a wealthy man. If George was involved, Dad reasoned, he would have the money to win.

Dad decided to invite Steinbrenner to be part of his group's attempt to buy the New York Yankees. However, George would have to put his money where his mouth was. Dad believed he had a strong enough rapport with Steinbrenner to let him in on the fact that he and a group of investor friends were planning to make a bid for the Yankees.

"What about the Yankees, George? I think the Yankees might be right for investment now," I can just hear Dad saying.

"The Yankees are for sale?" George asked quietly, raising his eyebrows.

"Not yet officially. Michael Burke and I talked some at the last meeting. CBS wants out. Burke says they want out of baseball, but he doesn't want to leave it."

Dad and Burke had talked. Michael said he believed CBS would move faster if they knew that Gabe was involved with the purchasing group. Gabe's investors did not object to Michael continuing to run the team. He was showy, but effective enough to have kept his baseball management job with the Yankees. Nevertheless, Dad knew that adding George to his group would be a tough sell to other prospective owners.

"I want in. I want in big, bigger than with the Indians," George said, animatedly.

"Not so fast," Dad said. "There are others in front of you, things we need to talk about with the group. We have our group together."

"Gabe, I don't want to wait. Nick got the team the last time I waited. Who is in, now?"

"I'm leading the group, George. They want me to run things more so than here," said Gabe.

Gabe filled in a few more holes without revealing too much. He told George that Steve O'Neill and members of the Broadway-savvy Nederlander family along with other prominent Clevelanders and New Yorkers had expressed strong interest in the Yankees. He confided to George that he had the financing to buy the team with his ownership group, but he needed more funds to pay for the level of skill he thought the Yankees needed to return to their glory days. Gabe told George that he did not want to be in the same situation that he was in with the Indians. There were times that as their general manager and owner that he did not have the money to pay salaries, buy balls, or turn on the lights. Gabe didn't like being forced to trade good players just to get by. Steinbrenner was interested, but for a price; he wanted to be the general partner.

"I know you know how to listen for the right opportunity, Gabe. I figured that out when you, Steve and Al and I talked to Vernon," George remarked.

Gabe smiled and said, "You're no jumping Jack, George. Notwithstanding what's been said and the history between you and Vernon's son, I believe that you have become a solid businessman. Rosen says you are for real."

"Listen to this, Gabe. I have the money I lined up for the Indians. I am not willing to be the second banana. I want to be the general partner of the LLP."

Gabe was not yet ready to concede. "Burke wants to be a general partner, too, and as I said, my investors want me to lead. Frankly, George, I don't think the others will go for it. They know what I bring." Gabe was hedging because he knew that George's proposal would cause trouble, but at the same time he needed George's money to succeed. His hesitancy fueled George's desire.

"Gabe, I have ideas, things I want to do. I can do it for Detroit."

"Yes, there is Detroit." Gabe smiled. "George, it's the Yankees."

"The Yankees. Yes it is, Gabe. They remind me of the Indians. No pennant for what how many years? They have our Nettles, now, don't they? Good one Gabe," he scowled.

"They won in 1964, George. The Yankees can win again, but we — the new owners — have to be ready to take a few chances," said Gabe.

"I am not afraid to take a gamble. I have the money to play like Mr. Big in Texas with a lot more business sense," George responded.

My dad answered, "Good. You will need it. Michael knows how to get it from other sources, too. It takes a lot of money to be a baseball team owner, George. Michael is the CEO now. He convinced the city to put up $27 million for stadium renovation and a lease that favors owners." It was a clear jab at Steinbrenner's pal, Modell.

"Take my offer to your investors Gabe. Tell them I can be a team player. I can get things done like Michael. I won't interfere with the operations, Gabe. I want to be the general partner. You can handle the business side. We all have our strengths," George said.

"I'll take it to them, George. I'll call Burke. I'll let you talk to him about your general partner request. He will want to know where he fits in if he gives in to that."

"You talk to the others Gabe. Let there be no doubt what I am offering here."

Dad wanted the authority to run the team his way. He also wanted to make sure that the jobs of general manager Lee MacPhail and manager Ralph Houk, men he respected for their strengths and ability, would be safe. Gabe knew it was important to the success of the deal.

George agreed to supply the working capital and give Gabe the freedom and authority to run the team and make the trades that he wanted in exchange for 15.5 percent of the team, with 3.5 percent specifically designated for his share of the LLP. The price proved irresistible to Dad who knew he could build a winner if he had the budget.

Despite resistance from members of the new limited partnership, Dad persuaded the group that he could do the work that needed to be done more effectively if he were out of the spotlight. The partners in the buying group expected Dad to be the one in charge, and they planned to invest in him and the Yankees. They had confidence in his character and ability. As expected, there was push back against George being the general partner; the objections were strong and the arguments many. Somehow, Gabe prevailed. He saw something he needed in George that the other partners did not - dollar signs! He was willing to fight for George even though it was clear that George did not know anything about baseball, while Dad had by that time more than 50 years of experience in the game.

The prospective owners from the Nederlander family pleaded with Gabe to stick with his plan to be the general partner, rather than give in to Steinbrenner's demands. In fact, the Nederlanders pushed back the hardest. I know that Dad and Steve O'Neill were great friends and they talked about George's involvement more than the others in the group did. (Memories of the conversations, recounted over the years by some of the great men in baseball and in discussions with my brothers, came together as I read Dad's personal files.)

"Gabe, no. When we said we were in, we meant we were behind you. You know the business and the game," Nederlander said. "I heard about the way George does business. I don't like what I hear," he added.

One investor and long-time Cleveland man complained, "George has not done a particularly good job as the lead man for the Pipers."

"He does not know anything about baseball, and I am not sure what he knows about shipbuilding, given what has happened with the company since he took over the helm," scoffed a close friend.

Dad responded, "Vernon didn't know much about baseball when he first came, either. But I was here. We did okay before the money problems and other issues came up. When George was interested in buying the team from Vernon, you were in, Steve. You trusted my judgment."

"I knew you would be running things here. New York? I don't know," Steve said.

"I'll be making the trades, building the team and getting the numbers in line with our goal to win. I'll be there, Steve."

"MacPhail and Burke are good people Gabe," Nederlander added.

"Lee is my friend. Burke knows the numbers on the Yankees," Dad said. He had genuine affection for these men he respected. Dad knew he was winning.

"The Yankees are a financial drain on CBS. They lost $11 million in the last eight years, but Michael reduced this debt to $5 million. I can do more. My office will be alongside George's. I'll be where I can do the most good with the numbers we bring in," said

Gabe. "A team has to have money to operate. You saw what it was like here. We didn't win."

"We lost more than games when Vernon and Alvin Dark got out of hand," said O'Neill. "I don't want to go there again. Stouffer had a point about George running Cleveland, Gabe."

"George is a complex businessman, Steve. You know he paid the bills for the Pipers in the end to spare the other nine owners from owning a bankrupt team."

"Some question his motives and sources."

"He has people and banks lining up to give him money. That could come in handy, Steve. I think we can protect ourselves from the other risks," Dad said to Steve and the others. Soon after, Dad put George in touch with Michael, and the three men came together with a sincere interest in developing the winning bid.

In the first bid, these power players reasoned that CBS would be glad to get out of the subsidiary running the Yankees and instead focus on the business of broadcasting, their forte. Michael Burke in 1964 had convinced CBS to buy the Yankees when he was in charge of subsidiary acquisition. CBS owner William Paley was never fully onboard, though Michael spent eight years working to retain his interest. By the fall of 1972, Michael was sure CBS was about done. The original documents in Dad's files include both the preliminary bid for $4.5 million, and the final one that CBS would accept for $10 million in February 1973. The network bought two parking garages back shortly thereafter, bringing the actual out of pocket costs down to $8.8 million.

For the other partners, the possibility of owning a winner run by Gabe Paul, a proven quantity, made it easy to overlook the threat hidden in George Steinbrenner's involvement.

Steinbrenner's reputation as a hothead when he owned the Pipers preceded him; one reporter commented that he felt George was psychologically unfit to own a sports team. The fact that George Steinbrenner was considered a risk factor during the due diligence report put together for the potential investors was largely unknown by Yankee fans and followers. Dad's personal files include a memorandum dated February 14, 1973, and under "other factors" it states:

> Although Michael Burke and Gabe Paul have been active in the operations of a professional baseball club, George Steinbrenner, although previously an investor in other professional sports teams, has had no prior experience in the management of an operation comparable to the Yankees.

Nevertheless, Gabe made a strong case for what George's business capabilities could bring as the general partner with Michael and Lee in place. The investors in the original ownership group knew Gabe Paul. With Dad committing to use his experience to guide the organization and operation, the sales pitch proved irresistible to New York and Cleveland's elite. Dad said, "I have that all worked out in the New York partnership agreement."

Dad knew that bringing George in to the Yankee ownership group meant the opportunity to operate at an unprecedented level. It also brought back memories of the peril involved in collaborating with risk-takers who loved the game and hated to lose. Dad knew more about the business of baseball than anyone in the game, but George was shrewd. With the assistance of lawyers and Gabe's knowledge of these past agreements, they drew up a preliminary MOU (memorandum of understanding) for prospective team owners. It included a clause which was a clear warning from Gabe and the legal experts that the general partner did not know much about baseball. Signing the agreement to become an owner meant accepting this business opportunity and the risk that came with it.

Gabe Paul's certified check for purchase of
an interest in the New York Yankees

FORM OF ACCEPTANCE

OF

SUBSCRIPTION AGREEMENT

The Subscription Agreement, dated 19th March, 1973 submitted by [or on behalf of] Gabriel Paul subscribing for 5 Units of Partnership Interests in New York Yankees Partnership is hereby accepted pursuant to the terms and conditions thereof.

Dated as of: NEW YORK YANKEES PARTNERSHIP

March 22, 1973   By _____
                     General Partner

Acceptance of Gabe's subscription for an interest
in the New York Yankees partnership

In retrospect, George outsmarted everyone. The press announcement indicated that all the owners would be equal partners and that the current management with MacPhail and Houk would remain the same. Neither of these statements would prove to be the reality that the investors had signed on for.

SCHEDULE A

NEW YORK YANKEES PARTNERSHIP

A LIMITED PARTNERSHIP

NAME AND ADDRESS	PARTNERSHIP PERCENTAGE
(GENERAL PARTNER)	
George M. Steinbrenner III c/o Investment Plaza - Suite 1210 1801 East Ninth Street Cleveland, Ohio 44114	15.5 (including 3.5 limited partner interest)
(LIMITED PARTNERS)	
1. James M. Nederlander (shared interest) 5523 East Arroyo Road Scottsdale, Arizona 85251	2.50
(a) Harry Nederlander 704 North Woodward Avenue Birmingham, Michigan 48011	1.25
(b) Joseph Z. Nederlander 24545 Mulberry Drive Southfield, Michigan 48075	2.50
(c) Fred R. Nederlander 27431 Willow Green Court Franklin, Michigan 48025	1.25
(d) Robert E. Nederlander 4616 Private Lake Drive Birmingham, Michigan 48010	2.50
2. F. J. (Steve) O'Neill (shared interest)	

Original partnership document — page 1 of 4

NAME AND ADDRESS	PARTNERSHIP PERCENTAGE
(a) John Andrew Kundtz, Trustee U/T/A Dated September 29, 1972 F/B/O F. J. O'Neill National City Bank Building East 6th Street & Euclid Avenue Cleveland, Ohio 44114	5.00
(b) Albert L. Rosen 200 National City Bank Building East 6th Street & Euclid Avenue Cleveland, Ohio 44113	1.00
(c) John Andrew Kundtz and Henry A. Zimmerman, Trustees U/T/A May 24th, 1972 F/B/O W. J. O'Neill National City Bank Building East 6th Street and Euclid Avenue Cleveland, Ohio 44114	4.00
3. Daniel R. McCarthy (shared interest) 962 Illuminating Building Cleveland, Ohio 44113	3.00
Edward M. Greenwald 962 Illuminating Building Cleveland, Ohio 44113	3.00
4. Thomas W. Evans 133 East 64th Street New York, New York 10021	2.00
5. Charlotte L. Witkind 256 South Colombia Avenue Columbus, Ohio 43209	3.00
6. Gabriel Paul 23500 Standford Road Shaker Heights, Ohio 44122	5.00
7. Jess A. Bell 18519 Detroit Avenue Lakewood, Ohio 44107	7.00

Original partnership document — page 2 of 4

3

NAME AND ADDRESS	PARTNERSHIP PERCENTAGE
8. Marvin L. Warner Highland Towers 1071 Celestial Street Cincinnati, Ohio 45202	10.00
9. Lester Crown (shared interest) 300 West Washington Street Chicago, Illinois 60606	.50

(a) John J. Crown
    300 West Washington Street
    Chicago, Illinois 60606
	5.00

(b) Arie Steven Crown
    300 West Washington Street
    Chicago, Illinois 60606
	.50

(c) Benjamin Z. Gould, Trustee
    James S. Crown Trust
    U/T/A 12-30-57
    300 West Washington Street
    Chicago, Illinois 60606
	.50

Patricia A. Crown Trust U/T/A 12-30-57	.50
Daniel M. Crown Trust U/T/A 12-30-57	.50

(d) Harry N. Wyatt, Trustee
    Sara B. Crown Trust
    U/T/A 6-2-60
    300 West Washington Street
    Chicago, Illinois 60606
	.50

David A. Crown Trust U/T/A 1-22-63	.50
William H. Crown Trust U/T/A 7-30-63	.50
Susan Crown '65 Trust U/T/A 12-28-65	.50
Janet S. Crown '65 Trust U/T/A 12-28-65	.50

Original partnership document— page 3 of 4

```
                                                          4

NAME AND                          PARTNERSHIP
ADDRESS                           PERCENTAGE

10. Edward Ginsberg
    650 Terminal Tower
    Cleveland, Ohio 44113             5.00

11. Sheldon B. Guren
    650 Terminal Tower
    Cleveland, Ohio 44113             5.00

12. N. Bunker Hunt
    2700 First National Bank Bldg.
    Dallas, Texas 75202               5.00

13. Michael Burke
    145 West 58th Street
    New York, New York 10006          5.00

14. John Z. DeLorean
    P. O. Box 427
    Bloomfield Hills, Michigan 48013  1.00

15. Leslie Combs II
    Spendthrift Farm
    P. O. Box 996
    Lexington, Kentucky 40501          .50
```

Original partnership document — page 4 of 4

Gabe Paul was on the books for five percent. George Steinbrenner and Michael Burke were introduced as the team's general partners, and Gabe was identified to the media as a more active owner by George Steinbrenner. In truth, George was the only general partner. The media had misunderstood, it turned out, as had Burke. Burke retained his operational role as the CEO and secured five percent ownership when CBS sold the team to Gabe's group for $10 million. The newspapers reported it took only three days to move from the offer to a signed deal. The newspapers do not always get it right. There were earlier offers that did not make their way into the press. As a reporter and an insider, I have learned that real life is always bigger than the leaks and the official press release.

Yankees ownership group 1973

When Dad made the announcement, Burke and Steinbrenner stood behind him or alongside him, depending on your perspective. This partnership that began with fanfare and apparent good will already contained the seeds of discord that would grow into future headaches and headlines.

In addition to Gabe, Michael and George, the signed ownership documents from Dad's files identify the other members of the limited liability partnership.

- o The Nederlander family of Broadway fame with a 10 percent interest that was shared among James Nederlander, Harry Nederlander, Joseph Nederlander, Fred Nederlander, and Robert Nederlander.
- o Francis J. "Steve" O'Neill shared 10 percent with John Andrew Kundtz, Al Rosen, and Henry Zimmerman, all of Cleveland, Ohio.
- o Daniel R. McCarthy, also of Cleveland, shared his 6 percent interest with another Clevelander, Edward Greenwald.
- o New Yorker Thomas Evans had 2 percent.
- o Federated Department Stores (Bloomingdales and Lazarus) bigwig Charlotte Witkind, who always came with her delightful husband Dick, held 3 percent.
- o Another Clevelander, Jess Bell, the Bonnie Bell make-up guy had 7 percent.
- o Marvin Warner, from Ohio Title, later appointed Ambassador to Switzerland during Jimmy Carter's administration, bought 10 percent.
- o Lester Crown, a Chicago businessman, shared his 10 percent interest with John Crown, Arie Steven Crown, Benjamin Gould (a trustee for James Crown), Patricia Crown, Daniel Crown, and Harry Wyatt, a trustee for Sara Crown, David Crown, William Crown, Susan Crown, and Janet Crown.
- o Edward Ginsberg of Cleveland was in for 5 percent.
- o Sheldon B. Guren of Cleveland also had 5 percent.
- o Nelson Bunker Hunt, one of the Hunt brothers from Texas, had 5 percent.
- o The car magnate John DeLorean had 1 percent.
- o Horseracing's Leslie Combs II, founder of Kentucky's Spendthrift Farms, had .50 percent.

New York Yankees Partnership other than Gabe Paul, Michael Burke, and George Steinbrenner

While Dad was building an ownership group, I was studying full time at the American University and working part time under Shirley Povich at *The Washington Post*. As the first woman in the sports department I was under a lot of pressure, and to get away from it all sometimes I would take a drive. One day, I was enjoying the scenic horse country in Middleburg, Virginia. On my way back to D.C. I stopped for a soda and decided to call home from the pay phone at the country store.

I barely said "Hello" when Mom blurted out, "Jennie, we have some news for you!"

I waited. I never knew what to expect from Mom.

"We are moving to New York. Your father just bought the New York Yankees. Your father will be glad to see you and tell you all about it when you come home."

I wasn't so sure about that. When I first got my job at *The Washington Post*, I thought Dad would be proud. I thought we would have something that finally we could talk about, even though I was more interested in the human interest side of a story than the numbers and statistics that he loved. He just loved to talk about baseball.

Because of Dad, I always seemed to know what was going on before the newspapers. I got the scoop when I realized that the floor vent in my room was directly over Dad's office in our Cleveland home. Dad's diary included an account where he had his staff plug up the vents at the stadium office in order to keep his trading moves and deals quiet. If he had only known how clearly everything came through the vent between his home office and my room.

I could hear everything that Dad said late at night in his office. That is also how I learned that my dad was often silent about the fact that he was born of Russian Jewish immigrant parents. We were raised with Mom's religion, and when his dinner guests commented on the fine Episcopal upbringing of my brothers and me, Dad said little about his faith.

I started to pay closer attention to how much baseball meant to Dad. When Dad would stay up until all hours of the night making trades, so would I. My ear was glued to the vent. I heard what he went through to get Rocky Colavito back in Cleveland, and who it cost him. I knew how many people wanted to move the Indians to their town. It is also the way I discovered that some of his peers and a few beat reporters called him "the Smiling Cobra."

I didn't know what they meant then, or that it might have been an indicator of what was to come in our relationship when he bought the Yankees. Later, I realized that his enemies nicknamed him the Smiling Cobra when they experienced the surprise of a loss made more shocking because it came from a source they did not expect. He wanted to win, and he had no problem using surprise as a tactic. I believe the reason Dad did what he did was fear and an intense need for self preservation. I believe my father's true character was as a smart, loving, introspective man who did the best he could. It would take me many years to understand that. While the truth did set me free, first it would hurt.

Dear Dad,

People still ask me the same question, today. They want to know what it was like to be your daughter when you turned the New York Yankees around and pushed them to become champions again. Do you know what I tell them, Dad? From the moment that Mom gave me the news, I knew my life would be anything but normal.

When you bought the Yankees, I was so happy and proud of you. I was sincerely beaming for your success and the fact that the future you dreamed of was actually here. What happened over the five years that you owned this team — and in its aftermath — was a watershed for America's favorite pastime, as well as for you and me. You did so much for the team, and so much for me...and to me. I loved it and I hated it at the same time. Under your guidance and control, the New York Yankees went from doormats to champions in less than three years. It was the other way around for me and you, Dad.

The fact that I have yet to resolve the challenges of our relationship makes me question why we both fell short of the other's expectations. Everybody loved you for what you did. Mom thought you were right as did so many others, including the boys. As for me Dad, I hated you for it at first. Then I loved you. Sometimes, Dad, I felt both emotions at the same time as that gap between what I wanted and what I had became a bigger and bigger daddy hole.

I hated that I always had to share you with everyone at work, and yet I loved that a baseball stadium was my playground. I loved that people referred to you, my dad, as amazing. Just like all the other people in baseball that always seemed to be around, I admired you so, Dad. Did you know that? I tried to tell you in all those letters that I wrote to you. But I couldn't tell how you felt. Your letters were missing something. Perhaps you kept your feelings out of the letters you dictated to your secretary.

I still miss you, Dad.

Love, Jennie

3
Baseball and Politics Don't Mix

Baseball in the 1970s was one of the few places during that tumultuous decade where being old school was still an edge. As Phil Pepe wrote, "That's when the old, yet untarnished thrill of being a Yankee was every boy's dream." Sticking by George despite pressure from the other owners to take the helm instead of giving it to the Cleveland shipbuilder allowed Gabe to keep his word and establish himself in a position of strength. Ensuring a steady flow of cash into the new organization appeared to be a good decision for Dad and his New York Yankees...and it was initially. The Yankees now had tradition, money, and Gabe Paul — three elements that are still associated with success in baseball all these years later.

When Dad's ownership team took over, the Yankees were losing money. George agreed to bankroll a return to a healthy bottom line that delivered higher attendance as long as he could do it his way. In the beginning George's way was Dad's way, just like Dad told the other owners it would be. Dad was in control of the way the Yankees would emerge, he thought. I believe that he felt the same way about me. Both of these perceptions would be challenged before the year was over.

Major league baseball rules prevented ownership in two teams because of potential conflict of interest. Dad had an ownership in the Indians but had to place it in an escrow account so that it could be sold. Having cleared almost a million dollars on the Mileti purchase of the Indians, my dad had the money to play with the best of them. His long time friend Steve O'Neill wanted to support Gabe in this dream venture, but he also wanted some assurance that Gabe would not be lost to Clevelanders forever. Their discussions would play a pivotal role in Dad's field of dreams and in a few nightmares for us both.

Dad and Steve came to a gentlemen's agreement regarding their commitment to Cleveland. If Mileti turned out to be a disaster and if the Indians needed Steve to rescue the franchise, Gabe told his friend that he would return to Cleveland to help him do that. Until then, Gabe would leave his heart in Cleveland and go to New York.

Gabe's financial position with the Yankees was hard earned and he wanted to keep what he had. To do that, he reasoned, he needed George, who was clearly hungry for his next big game. Dad knew that George had been bankrupt before with the Pipers and had come back. Dad knew George was a high-stakes gambler. The idea of losing everything was not a roadblock to George. As a first generation American, Dad had a different outlook on money, life's responsibilities, and the American way. He was a realist who felt he had to protect himself and his investors from George.

Remembering the past, Gabe saw to it that the agreement protected the other owners from anyone who failed to come up with the money needed for the team. The language was written to include all owners, but it was clearly directed toward George, and it stemmed from Dad's experience with Vernon Stouffer who had promised so much and delivered so little. In brief, it forced a two-for-one forfeiture of an owner's percentage if an owner could not meet a cash call equal to his present stake in the team. The forfeit share would be sold to secure the revenue, if needed, without forcing a sale of the team. The Yankees had the first right of refusal subject to the percent that they controlled at that time. Although

George had a 3.5 percent limited partner interest in the Yankees in the beginning, as general partner, he controlled 15.5 percent. The general partner could block the sale of stock to outsiders. The final agreement included these subtle protections against the arrangements that in the past had tied the hands of the Indians LLP. George's lawyers managed to tuck in other broad language, which allowed the general partner to borrow money from the Yankees to pay for forfeited shares. As general partner he could issue cash calls, and they came more frequently than many of the owners expected and could afford. In this way George steadily increased his share of the Yankees.

At the time, Michael Burke and Gabe were confident that including the clause was the right thing to do for the Yankees, and that it would protect the key members of the group. The language was tactical. George saw it as a way to gain control of the Yankees, and he would use it like a sledgehammer. His use of this clause would ultimately put Gabe in a very difficult position. But it would happen to Burke first. If either man considered the probability of this turn of events, they dismissed it as the ink dried on the paperwork to buy the Yankees. Others would suffer before it would affect Gabe directly.

Dad thought he was avoiding a risk in the future by saying something smart in the present. He did not anticipate that George had a mean curve ball and would use it on him. This pattern showed up in my relationship with Dad, too; Dad and I were very much alike although neither one of us knew it at that time.

George Steinbrenner promised that little would change in the New York Yankee organization except for their losing streak. At the press conference following the purchase, George said that he would be a behind-the-scenes boss. "Gabe Paul," he said, "will be the administrative partner and a more active owner. His addition will not affect Lee MacPhail, the current Yankee GM, or manager Ralph Houk. It's not a front office shake-up. Gabe will assist Michael Burke, the NY Yankee President in the operation of team. Things will move forward as before, with a deep sense of regard for Yankee tradition. Nobody tampers with that tradition."

Nobody that is except George Steinbrenner and some of the people who were invited to sit in his box over the years. The first unexpected change came within a few months when in April of 1973 Michael Burke was ousted from his role of president.

Burke had been effective at negotiating a good lease with the city of New York, a business skill that Dad respected. Dad could have arranged for a new lease given the ownership change but he recommended that George honor the existing lease, and he did. That decision would be very financially advantageous to the Yankees particularly after the 1977 World Series when their payout to the city was miniscule compared to the revenues generated.

Dad's and Burke's personalities, goals, and operating styles clashed in ways that surprised Dad. According to Dad's diary, he was focused on getting the numbers to work for the team, while Michael was more interested in keeping things as they were. Burke had respected Dad as a lifelong baseball businessman. Five years before, Gabe had spearheaded a move to make Burke the commissioner of baseball when CBS owned the "Bronx Bombers." (Bowie Kuhn got the job instead.)

Dad liked the cooperative, friendly spirit of the team in place, and at the same time resented some excesses and flamboyance. It was reminiscent of his experience in Cleveland and Houston. Now, Dad and Michael were both active owners of the Yankees, with George. The other limited partners were not involved in the team. Dad once commented that working together day in and day out revealed that Burke's operating style was more consistent with his earlier careers as a secret agent, circus director, and film writer.

Burke's way of doing business was in sharp contrast to Dad's more conventional, low-key style. Steinbrenner and Dad found themselves disagreeing with a number of judgments that Burke made. Steinbrenner objected to the way Michael spent money on player contracts and office decorations. In addition, the cost over-runs on the stadium renovation mounted, and other expenditures exceeded expectations, resulting in a cash call just three months after the ownership change. Gabe covered his cash call with future deferred salary payments, which he had negotiated into his contract. Burke, though, could not meet the financial obligations of the call. It was the first of many cash calls that would anger the limited partners, including Dad's dear friends and supporters in the Nederlander family.

The clause that Dad engineered into the ownership agreement to protect him and owners from a potential financial disaster with George had instead presented an unanticipated solution to an escalating conflict among the three men. After a couple of weeks of silence, Steinbrenner and Burke jointly announced Burke's resignation due to "differences in business operating philosophies" that could not be resolved in a way that allowed the business relationship to continue in its current manner.

There was speculation that Dad and George had planned to move Burke out from the beginning. Burke dodged this question deftly in a five-paragraph prepared statement distributed before a doubleheader. At the press conference, it was clear that the bitterness he often wrote and talked about years later was not evident that day. On that day, the conversations were very different — upbeat yet guarded.

"Our first interest is the good of the Yankees," said Burke, who had run the Yankees for the eight years prior. "I would have preferred a different outcome but after some rocky times that George and I had together, I am personally delighted that we have resolved our differences on a friendly basis."

Burke agreed to continue as a consultant for the next ten years and a limited partner with a small percentage of the club, which was far below the five percent that was originally on the books for him. When asked why Mike left, Dad sidestepped this issue like the consummate PR man he was. "Only Mike can answer that. This is something conceived and generated by Mike." Outsiders thought Dad was talking about the new reduced role and consultant/ownership agreement. Those on the inside knew that Dad was also referring to the initial clause Burke helped Dad put into the partnership agreement.

Dad was asked to comment on speculation that Burke had not put up the money for his stake in the club, and in fact was given shares in Dad's bidding group early on for the role he played in making the deal happen. Dad refused to add anything to that potential wildfire, which could have spread a bit close to home. Instead, he quelled it quickly with the words the press corps needed and little more. "As far as I know, Burke had money in the club. He is listed as purchasing shares," Dad said.

"When you're so totally immersed in something like the Yankees there's a certain lingering sadness or disappointment when things don't turn out well. But one has to be pragmatic," remarked Burke. Much later, Michael publicly lashed out at Dad for pushing him out.

Dad avoided getting personal. "We've got to have a sound business operation. The most important thing is what happens on the field, but it all depends on a sound operation. You've got to blend the two into a successful entity," said Gabe.

The talk that followed was about which persons fit best into which areas, a comment that started quite a few conversations on where Dad would fit into the organization when it all settled out. Sports beat reporters considered Lee MacPhail's job as general manager to be the one to be in jeopardy. Steinbrenner meanwhile said he did not intend to tell Dad or Lee how to run the club. "Some people may find it hard to believe," the shipping magnate commented, "but I don't intend to project myself into it. They will see no interference from me. I think we have it working now in a way that will be best for the Yankees, with Gabe's background and experience, he couldn't join an organization like this without getting involved," continued George.

Like the other woman who believes that she will be different from the last woman her man cheated on, Dad bought that. So did Lee MacPhail. Dad's diary echoed his belief in George's declaration that he would stay out of the club operations. Dad wrote, "Lee will remain as general manager in charge of baseball operations, while I handle company business, and Ralph Houk, the best manager in baseball, will run the team. No radical changes are planned in presenting the team to the public. The major changes will be in the running of the club as a business. I want to turn it around."

Many people do not realize the extensive business side of a baseball team from logistics, to production, to press relations, to player strategy and trading; it all fell on Gabe Paul when Michael Burke left.

Dad's new secretary, Pearl Davis, was a gem and they got on fabulously from the beginning. I loved Pearl, too, right from the start. She was older than I was by a few years, and the first black woman I ever met in such a high position. Pearline Davis, Executive Secretary to Howard Berk, Michael Burke, and Gabe Paul of the New York Yankees from 1968–1978 calls herself "…the gal from Harlem who walked across the 155th Street bridge and fell in love with the 'Bronx Bombers,' my own N.Y. Yankees, the best team in the whole wide world."

Pearl loved the stadium and knew everything about the people that came and went in that office and the locker room. She did not know as much as Dad did about the game, although she was amazingly knowledgeable about her beloved Yankees. The team, the staff, the secretaries, they were like family to her. She looked out for Dad, too. George did not like that; Dad tried to protect her from George's anger.

I asked Pearl about their relationship after I began looking through Dad's diary and she filled in some of the gaps.

After your Dad and George came, everything changed. There was a lot of yelling. People lost their jobs over a sandwich, and they were scared. In my view, the new owners were about dividing and conquering the veterans and the people who knew how to get things done. Later, I saw that Mr. Steinbrenner was often in the middle of a conversation that would break a staffer down until they became intimidated or stayed silent. I saw him do it a lot to the secretaries, to his staff, to his manager. I saw him do it to my boss, Mr. Gabe Paul. I have met all kinds of people in my life, the good, the bad, the ugly, and then there are the special ones like Gabe you never forget. He was my boss, like my father at times, and most of all my best friend, who protected me and he knew that I protected him in return.

I fought most of my battles on my knees. I didn't ask questions. I didn't get stuck in the "why's" that hold so many people back. I just got up and got involved. I looked out for the team I loved. There was a lot of shouting, although it came from George, not from Gabe. He would sit there and take it. Then Gabe would offer his wisdom or say his piece. Mr. Steinbrenner would listen, sometimes, and they would agree to something. The next day, the story would be different, and Gabe would be the fall guy, forced to clean up the difficulty. I didn't understand why Mr. Steinbrenner did that. One had the money. One had the brains. Mr. Steinbrenner always surrounded himself with people that were good at what they did. Your Dad was one of those people, Jennie, and he did not get the credit for all he did or what he knew or the important trades he made early on in the game.

Dad's office was next to George's, separated only by a thin door. The two owners talked regularly about the team that they would make winners again on the field and on the balance sheet. Meanwhile, as Dad's role continued to grow and he and George inserted themselves in more and more decisions affecting the team, the leaders of the past followed Burke out the door, starting with MacPhail. Without Burke as a buffer between the new management and the establishment, Lee experienced what it was like to work for "the boss" who second-guessed and criticized the knowledgeable people. It was difficult to tell if the pressure was coming from George or Gabe at first. Dad respected Lee and then stepped into his shoes, taking over Lee's responsibilities. Dad defended George and gave Lee credit for a good trade in Lou Piniella as a farewell move. It would be an excellent move for the home team and allow MacPhail, a well regarded, highly accomplished farm director-to-GM baseball success story, to leave a positive legacy for the Yanks.

Dad was surprised when George continued to attempt to dissuade him from the baseball moves, which he thought were clearly discussed and decided. At about that same time, the Yankees started to lose. Manager Ralph Houk was under pressure. He had a hard time with the fans' lack of support after a 35-year tenure that included a few championships early on. George was angry. When Houk decided to resign from the Yankees, George tried to get him to stay even as Gabe attempted to entice Oakland A's manager Dick Williams to leave Charlie Finley. Houk went to Detroit, but a tampering charge would derail the Yankee plan for his replacement. Gabe went after Bill Virdon as the manager instead. George balked on the deal in a tirade hours before, but Dad went ahead with it anyway. It was a test of wills and authority. This time, as he would on so many occasions, George would acquiesce and return to good-natured support for my dad. The Yankees had a new manager and the beginning of a love-hate relationship between the general partner and my dad, a not-so-limited partner.

Things were heating up. The Yankees played like 1973 would be the year that they finally might turn things around. It was as though people sensed that history was about to be made, even though no one but Gabe saw it like it would be. He was a visionary, no doubt about it. Everybody wanted to be at the Stadium, including the Nixons. In the news even more than the Yankees in 1973, the first family's daughter Tricia and her husband needed a break from the Watergate spotlight and the questions of the press. When George Steinbrenner said he wanted to show respect for the President of the United States and at the same time to give them a day off from the media blitz, Dad could relate. He was willing to do whatever it took to make this powerful man's family feel at home in the owners' suite.

George's name surfaced in the infamous Watergate investigation because he was accused of making illegal contributions to Richard Nixon's 1972 campaign fund. He allegedly forced American Ship Building Company employees to make personal contributions from money they received through the company, and later to lie about it, obstructing the investigation. (In 1974 he was indicted on 14 counts and pleaded guilty to making illegal campaign contributions and obstruction. Bowie Kuhn suspended him from baseball for two years, later reduced to nine months.)

Dad now was doing the job of three men, while trying to placate Joan Steinbrenner and many of the general partners who suffered from the fallout of George's actions. The loud public fights between him and his wife made things more difficult; George even barred his wife from the dining room of the Stadium Club, and Dad was instructed to keep her away. At the same time, other owners were uncomfortable with George's high profile style that had brought negative attention to the team. Dad worked to keep the peace while George tried to maintain the facade of good relations with the press, the team, and his managers.

When the Nixon family wanted to come to the game, the special arrangements fell on Dad. He agreed to handle the details for the members of the First Family that afternoon in his ballpark. He promised to keep it low key and leveraged his relationships with reporters to ensure that there was no media coverage of their visit. Dad had to keep the reporters away from the box. The Yankees beat reporters did not like it; Dad did not give them a choice. He was very commanding and powerful himself. He silently implied that better stories would come to those who respected his authority and promise. He gave his word to the Nixons that there would be no media coverage, and he planned to keep it.

Dad invited me to be a companion for Tricia that day. It made sense to Dad for two young women to be together. I was the Yankee general manager's daughter, and Tricia and I were about the same age. It was not that he made an exception for me. I do not believe Dad even thought about my last two newspaper reporting jobs. The fact that I had recently left my job at the *Fort Lauderdale News* in Florida (which my editor at *The Washington Post* had arranged to give me more hard news experience) never came up. To Dad's way of thinking, it was a great afternoon at the ballpark with thousands of ordinary and not-so-ordinary people enjoying America's favorite pastime.

I think Dad included me because he thought Tricia would have a better time if she had someone like her nearby. Growing up with a baseball executive and team owner as a Dad exposes a daughter to a lot of relationship challenges with peers and strangers who think that they want to be you. They usually settled for the next best thing — getting close to my dad through me. Tricia understood that better than most. Having grown up with a famous father, she knew that sometimes people used you. It was a lot of pressure when your last name was Nixon in the early 1970s. It made our conversation easy. We shared an instant bond as two daughters with powerful and newsworthy fathers. The teams did not disappoint the fans watching that day; I would not do as well.

When Dad bought the Yankees, the number of people who wanted to get something for nothing from me got a whole lot worse. I didn't always know where people were coming from. I was not as good yet at reading people as my dad was; maybe I was not as good at listening as I thought either. I did not see that ball coming when Sheila Moran, a fellow woman reporter, called me up that night after the game. We were girlfriends on the surface, really more like well-behaved acquaintances. When Sheila called and asked me about the game, I just chatted away, like I would have with any other person. She asked a lot of questions about what Tricia and I did. I was not really paying attention.

I said silly things: "We just ate peanuts and popcorn. We had a hot dog, watched the game, the usual ballgame things."

She asked me, "Jennie, what did Tricia do when they flashed the President's name on the scoreboard and everyone booed?"

I thought that was a mean, catty thing to say. Tricia and I had bonded, and I didn't want to say anything personal about her or her Dad. I didn't answer. Sheila kept trying to get details. When I stopped giving information, Sheila seemed to lose interest, but a few minutes later, I realized that was not so.

"Jennie, why don't you write a story on it? I'll give it to my editor. We can work together here at the New York Post. It will be fun."

"Sheila, no way," I said. "This was a social thing and besides there is no story. I am not doing that to Tricia!"

"Jennie, everything is a story with the Nixons," Sheila said. "Do you mind if I write the story?"

"I don't want anything to do with this, Sheila. Whatever you do is your business."

"Okay, Jennie, I guess you're right. There isn't anything to write."

When we finally hung up, I was glad the conversation was over. I didn't know Sheila very well, but I really never thought it would be in the newspaper.

Foul tip! I was wrong. The day after Tricia's visit, the *New York Post* had a story on my afternoon with the President's daughter in George Steinbrenner's box at Yankee Stadium.

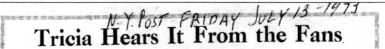

N.Y. POST FRIDAY JULY 13-1973

Tricia Hears It From the Fans

By SHEILA MORAN

Tricia Nixon Cox didn't mind the catcalls directed at the Kansas City Royals during last night's Yankees' game, but she gave her husband an exasperated look when when the fans roundly booed after her own name lit up on the scoreboard.

"Well, you can't win them all," Edward Cox said to her, according to one of their companions in the Presidential box at Yankee Stadium.

The couple watched the Yankees' 10-3 victory from a special enclosed section above the first-base line. The crowd of 18,000 didn't know the President's daughter was in the stadium until the sixth inning, when the scoreboard lit up with "Welcome Tricia Nixon Cox and Edward Cox."

According to Jennie Paul, daughter of Yankee President Gabe Paul, club officials phoned into the box for Tricia's permission to have the scoreboard announcement made. Tricia replied, "That would be very nice," Miss Paul said.

Toward the end of the game, an announcement of some sort was made in the press box. Tricia Nixon appeared not to hear it fully and, according to Miss Paul, asked her husband: "Is that about my father's pneumonia?"

Miss Paul said that except for that reference, Tricia did not discuss her father's illness. She also made no mention of Watergate.

The President's daughter, according to Miss Paul, is a knowledgeable baseball fan. She noticed the Yankees' hitting sensation, Ron Blomberg, was limping from a pulled leg muscle and mentioned that she had noticed the limp in a prior game.

Tricia was brought a hot dog, a soda and a bag of Pepperidge Farm oatmeal cookies by an usher during the game as well as an autographed Yankee baseball wrapped in a napkin. She clapped politely after each of the Yankees' 17 hits.

Associated Press Photo
Thurman Munson slides home, courtesy of a Gene Michael hit, while Royals' Fran Healey awaits throw.

Sheila Moran's story

Dad was livid. The story had little in it; what followed had everything to do with trust, broken confidences, and consequences.

I thought Dad would be angry at Sheila — she did us both wrong. Sheila had recounted many of the personal conversations Tricia and I had about the game, citing me as the source. The fact that she quoted me in the article flew in the face of everything Dad stood for, his word, his honor, and his intense desire to keep his family separate from the business of the New York Yankees. Personally, I was mortified. I knew Tricia and her dad would be hurt.

For Dad, it was all about keeping his word to the Nixons and respecting the reporters working the beat. Having started his career there himself he had an affinity for these deadline-driven folks. He knew their plight. They knew his game situation, and for the most part they gave him the same courtesy. As a reporter myself, I knew how the other reporters felt. Nobody likes to be scooped, or in my case duped.

Maybe I should have expected it from Sheila, but I did not. Throwing the paper down on my bed in my parent's New York apartment where I was staying, I said out loud to the wall, "How did my name get in the paper?" I didn't realize Dad was standing there. When I saw him, I tried to tell him that Sheila had called me at home and had talked to me like a friend after the game. I felt I had to tell him everything. I wanted to shout from the top of the stands, "I did not know she was planning to print it!"

He was not listening. Dad told me how George had said, "I'm always putting out fires involving Jennie!" and then followed with his own harsh words of disappointment in me. There was a lot of backlash on him and lots of speculation. Media attention for a nothing story was the last thing President Nixon or his daughter needed or expected when they accepted Dad's invitation to the ballgame, he lectured.

I knew Dad was embarrassed. His word had been compromised by someone not in his control. The fact that it was an accident was irrelevant. Whenever I spoke, it seemed that Dad heard something else. I answered his questions, but he became more frustrated. I couldn't understand why Dad cared that there was a story about nothing.

Feeling like a woman of the world at age 22, I had no idea what it meant to be Gabe Paul's daughter in 1973 until that moment. Who was I to be getting so much attention for such innocuous language? I thought. Who was this man posing as my dad instead of joining forces with me to fight Sheila for a retraction or at least an apology!

He kept saying the fact that there was a story *was* the story. Neither Dad nor I understood what the other was saying, despite repetition of the questions and the answers. I only saw how he reacted to me.

Preparing to shrink from the situation, I said, "Dad, I am sorry you feel that way. I did not want this to happen. If you feel that strongly about it, I'll leave town."

"Oh no, you don't." Dad said. "Not before you personally apologize to every reporter."

"Apologize for what, Dad?" I answered back a bit more spirited than usual when Dad was in his command-and-control mode.

"I gave them my word, Jennie."

"Your word to whom, Dad?"

"To the reporters, George, Dick, Tricia's husband. My word is my bond," Dad said sternly as he had said to me so many times before.

I knew that, of course. My dad and I were each embarrassed in our own way; I felt about two feet tall. Not exactly a father-daughter moment of the year. Looking for someone to blame besides myself, I wanted to go after Sheila for writing that story with or without him. Still fired up, I turned to tell Dad that's what I was going to do.

Too late.

Dad handed me a statement that was anything but personal. Suddenly, Michael Burke and I had something in common besides our long hair. That day, I parroted the press release.

> I am sensitive to your plight as a reporter, and I am sorry that I used my position as Gabe's daughter in a social situation to get and give sensitive information to another reporter.

That statement was not how it was at all; and yet, Dad pressured me to go to each reporter working the Yankees beat after I read the statement. He did not give me a choice. Instead of fighting Sheila with me, my dad made the story about me. The PR department for the New York Yankees had written a statement that everyone knew was force-fed and regurgitated on demand. Dad could have stood by me and protected me or supported me in some way. I felt so alone standing in front of the entire group of beat reporters with whom he had relationships.

Dad said nothing when I was done. I did what I was told, and then I let the reporters know that this was the last time we would be talking. They would never see me again, I vowed.

Like the men and women in the ownership team who had joined my dad in believing that he would be the team's leader with their best interests at heart, I trusted that Dad would know what to do for me. But on that day in 1973 I felt deeply betrayed. I wondered why fathers and daughters in the same conversations and same experiences fail to understand one another. I was only 22 and still trying to figure out why I felt like I was left standing out in left field. It pulled at my heart when he let me limp away. I felt his disapproval, and I was embarrassed that the man who I thought was my biggest fan chose not to get it. For a short while, I did not give a damn.

Without another word, I went back to Ohio retreating to the place where I had traded my first passion of riding horses for sports reporting. It was there that I rediscovered my competitive spirit. If I had to start over somewhere, it made sense to me to return to my roots and a place that I had experienced success without support from my dad. I found a job working local sports for Si Burrick, the award-winning sportswriter and columnist, for the *Dayton Daily News*. Si helped me get back in the game.

Dear Dad,

No one said anything about me being a sacrifice player after you bought the Yankees. Obviously, it can be a benefit to have a team focus in the game, but when is it okay in a father-daughter relationship?

Did you know what it was like for me when that story broke? I felt as if Sheila had pushed me in a puddle when I was wearing my Sunday best. It was as though you turned around just as she scurried away and scolded me as if I was a little girl who had embarrassed you by misbehaving in front of everyone. I was over 20! I wanted to fight back with you at my side. I needed you to listen to me, not scold me.

Dad, this was the beginning of many experiences that I would have of people using me to get close to the Yankees. I figured it out, eventually....In hindsight, I know the beat reporters were thinking I got stories or was in a position that was just handed to me. I noticed how you did not stand by me when I read that statement. Why Dad? If you were trying to teach me about respect, it didn't work. My emotions were fragile, my self-esteem at a new low. I was between jobs and afraid for my future. I was having a really hard time.

Dad, I needed your help to understand what had just happened. As far as I knew, the only mistake I had made was getting too friendly with the media. Well, maybe that and thinking I could take a day off and just be like every other young woman. I trusted the wrong people. Didn't that ever happen to you?

I would have known you loved me if you just talked it out with me instead of making me regurgitate something that was not genuine. If you could have said, "Jennie, I have to work with these guys every day. My integrity is on the line. If they think I did not honor my word and showed favoritism to you on a story, it will not be good for you or me professionally. If people think you have an unearned edge born of entitlement, they will respect you less. If that advantage comes from a source that they have to trust they will also doubt my forthrightness later.

"I can't have that, Jennie. I know it's tough for you now, but putting their jealousy to rest will prove to everyone that you are willing to work for the story. I know you work hard. I have never doubted that. In the meantime, I have to be extra hard on you now so others will know it, too."

You didn't say much after you handed me that statement, even after I went back to Ohio. When we saw each other after the whole Sheila affair, you would never come right out and say what was on your mind. It drove me crazy the way you could be so stuck on your point of view. I wanted to yell, "Spit it out, Dad. What are you trying to tell me?" I just kept waiting. It would have been better if someone had said what no one had said — something like, "I love you." I do, Dad.

Jennie

Jennie at home c. 1953

4

Gabe Hooks Catfish Hunter

By the 1974 baseball season, George Steinbrenner was noticeably absent from the Yankees front office because of those illegal contributions to President Nixon's election campaign. George took the position that it was a bad decision which had occurred prior to him buying in to the Yankees and becoming their general partner. With no jail time to serve he felt he could focus on baseball, but Commissioner Bowie Kuhn had other ideas and the power to act. He suspended George from any business dealings with the Yankees for two years. George could participate socially only, and so he often made appearances for games.

With George, Michael Burke, and Lee MacPhail gone from the Yankee front office, Gabe Paul was effectively in charge of rebuilding the Yankees. The limited partners were excited about the possibilities as was Dad. The future looked bright for the Yanks as Gabe led the team and George was forced to abstain publicly from the team workings. Behind the scenes, though, Steinbrenner had much to say and seemed constantly to be calling Dad's phone at our home. Although Dad became the decision maker, he still discussed all his moves with George.

It was during this time that Gabe Paul engineered one of the biggest coups in baseball for the New York Yankees. He signed "Catfish" Hunter to a $3.75 million deal, beating out 22 other ball clubs vying for the same big catch. Many could have predicted this signing given Dad's trade history and with George Steinbrenner's wallet as bait.

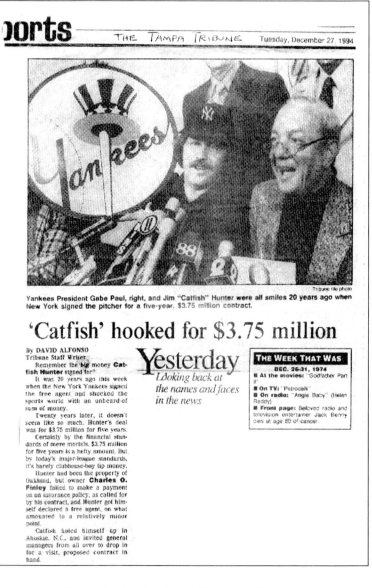

)orts — THE TAMPA TRIBUNE — Tuesday, December 27, 1994

Tribune file photo

Yankees President Gabe Paul, right, and Jim "Catfish" Hunter were all smiles 20 years ago when New York signed the pitcher for a five-year, $3.75 million contract.

'Catfish' hooked for $3.75 million

By DAVID ALFONSO
Tribune Staff Writer

Remember the big money Catfish Hunter signed for?

It was 20 years ago this week when the New York Yankees signed the free agent and shocked the sports world with an unheard-of sum of money.

Twenty years later, it doesn't seem like so much. Hunter's deal was for $3.75 million for five years.

Certainly by the financial standards of mere mortals, $3.75 million for five years is a hefty amount. But by today's major-league standards, it's barely clubhouse-boy tip money.

Hunter had been the property of Oakland, but owner **Charles O. Finley** failed to make a payment on an insurance policy, as called for by his contract, and Hunter got himself declared a free agent, on what amounted to a relatively minor point.

Catfish holed himself up in Ahoskie, N.C., and invited general managers from all over to drop in for a visit, proposed contract in hand.

Yesterday
Looking back at the names and faces in the news

THE WEEK THAT WAS
DEC. 26-31, 1974
■ At the movies: "Godfather Part II"
■ On TV: "Petrocelli"
■ On radio: "Angie Baby" (Helen Reddy)
■ Front page: Beloved radio and television entertainer Jack Benny dies at age 80 of cancer.

Remembering the Catfish Hunter deal of 1974

But in fact they almost missed landing Hunter when McDonald's founder and Padres owner Ray Kroc decided he wanted Catfish for San Diego, and bid $5 million. Before the negotiations were over, Dad and one of the limited partners, lawyer Ed Greenwald, convinced George to nearly double his initial offer, based on the advice of Clyde Kluttz, a former catcher and scout who knew Hunter and who was then working for the Yankees. For his part, the thought of being associated with a potential winner and a long line of players who made it into the Baseball Hall of Fame with the New York Yankees was more irresistible to Catfish than the Kroc's offer. He became the highest paid ballplayer on the roster of any team when he signed with the Yankees. For its time the deal was huge, and it was precedent-setting in the way the Yankees still buy players today. Compared to 21st century salaries at the Yankees, the money paid for Catfish may seem small. However, if you consider that Dad's salary was under $50,000 per year and he was an owner, general manager, and president, you get a feel for what it meant in its day.

My dad kept all the newspaper clippings from this famous deal in his diary. He wrote:

George told me we were not to back off in money deals, and when his unfortunate suspension was invoked, he told me 'anytime you have an opportunity to buy the contract of a player for cash, I want you to go ahead whenever in your judgment it would be advantageous to the Yankees.' This is the policy we followed in negotiating for Hunter. I remember I was personally thrilled to be operating under a program that permitted us to land a catfish. Delighted really to have completed negotiations to bring Jim (Catfish) Hunter to New York as a member of the Yankees.

More than a catalyst for a pennant winner and comeback, the Catfish deal was a milestone under the new free agency system that had evolved from a fight against the reserve clause. Dad had supported Hank Greenberg and Curt Flood in their precedent setting lawsuit that freed a player and his contract from a team at the end of their contract, which previously had not been the case. Before free agency, a team bought, sold, and negotiated packaged deals for players that they wanted, often as part of a more complex trade involving multiple players and many teams. It was all done with little regard to player preferences. At the end of a player contract, the club could automatically renew it or release the player; however, the team still owned the contract. Even after it expired, a new team had to buy out the contract.

Gabe Paul had done well under that old system. In fact, Dad was a shrewd trader with legendary success. He was known to do extensive research and then rely on his gut. At times, he traded on a hunch that someone he could get today would be the one he would need to make the deal later for the player he really wanted from an entirely different team. He also traded on principle, signing many of the first great black players in baseball despite rampant discrimination at the time. He would trade against his best judgment only when forced to for money, fan support, or ego, as he did with Rocky Colavito. His record with the Reds showed that Dad knew how to build pennant winners with players who made the difference, and he seized every opportunity to do so.

Supporting Curt Flood and Hank Greenberg would appear to be an unusual move for Dad who had built his fame on trades under the reserve clause system. Why would he do it? The short answer is that he stood up for what he believed in. It was not a question of personal connection to the Yankees or any players he knew who were involved. It was the principle that led Dad to fight the reserve clause publicly. When he understood that the reserve system in effect treated players as slaves and property, it stirred Dad's deepest conviction against discrimination, especially since he had also experienced discrimination of another kind in baseball.

So Gabe supported the end of the reserve system, and then worked the new system to his and the Yankees' advantage. According to former Yankees public relations man Marty Appel, "The arrival of free agency did not stop Gabe Paul. He was a man who built his career on what he did, whom he knew, and what he knew that you didn't. When free agency was the name of the game, Gabe Paul rolled up his sleeves and said, 'Deal me in.'" It would turn out to be the key to a winning strategy, which would reclaim the league pennant and the series for the Yankees after a 12-year dry spell.

Catfish was the first high-profile, high-dollar free agency deal that Dad made for the Yankees, a step toward his own dream of owning the number one team in baseball. It was also one of the many catalysts for a love-hate relationship with the New York Yankees, which fans, opponents, players, my father and I shared then and I still have today.

That Hunter was available at all was a fluke, and caused by a lapse that Charlie Finley could have avoided. The Cy Young Award-winning Catfish was a star performer for the Oakland A's, helping the team win with a 4-0 record in each of the 1972, 1973 and 1974 World Series. Then Finley, the man who had made his money in the insurance business, failed to make a $50,000 insurance payment on Catfish's policy, a major part of Hunter's contract with the A's. This contract breach resulted in Hunter being ruled a free agent. Courtesy of Dad and George Steinbrenner, his $100,000 A's salary would be replaced with a contract worth more than $3.75 million over five years.

The 1974 baseball season was full of surprises that would make Yankees history. By the time Catfish Hunter became available, Dad had already aided in a major reorganization of management and the line-up, trading Bobby Murcer for Bobby Bonds. Closing the Catfish Hunter deal just as the new year started set the tone for the future for the Yankees and my dad. It suddenly became clear that they could buy or trade anyone they needed.

Gabe Paul with Charlie Finley's mule, Charlie-O

That Gabe had lured Catfish Hunter away from Oakland A's owner and insurance magnate Charlie Finley was a bit of payback that somehow escaped the headlines of the day. Finley was the same man who had checked a mule into a Cleveland hotel under the name Gabe Paul several years before when Dad was still the general manager for the Indians. Finley thought he had the last laugh, despite the smile on Gabe's face in a photo taken in the hotel lobby, reins in hand. It was as if Dad already knew that he would get the last laugh one day. Charlie's stunt came back and bit him in the ass when Catfish became the New York Yankees' blue plate special.

Even after the Catfish deal, Dad insisted that the Yankees that he believed would one day win the World Series was not a purchased team. Dad maintained his investment and belief in the farm system, and it was still early in Dad's rebuilding efforts. When my dad courted Catfish, he had already signed Chris Chambliss and Dick Tidrow. Then when Gabe signed Catfish Hunter, everyone knew the times they were a-changing. They just did not know how much or what it would mean for baseball and the New York Yankees in the next few years.

With the Yankees in 1975, one reporter said, "If Gabe's player deals brought the New York Yankees to the brink of victory, the new era of free agency promised to push them over it." It would also drive up the price on players that few teams other than the New York Yankees, the Los Angeles Dodgers, and Boston Red Sox could afford.

Dad would love what free agency did for him as a Yankee owner, but in retirement, he would confess that he felt this change in the old school way of doing things had in fact ruined baseball. With it he got Catfish, a lot of great players, and unintended consequences for the Yankees. The price of good players was driven up by a feeding frenzy and Dad started it.

It was right about the time of the Catfish deal for Dad and the Yankees that I had discovered that my true passion was on-air reporting, and I moved to a job at the NBC affiliate in Cincinnati. I was excited by the continuous change of pace of on-air reporting, and I knew how to stick with it until I got the story. By this time in my fledgling career I had already achieved much more than many of my peers by following Dad's work ethic. When the cameras were off, I was even more focused. If there was something that I wanted, I did not back off. I went straight to the top.

I saw the job as a stepping-stone to the CBS network in New York, which was the number one network at the time. I called Robert "Bob" Wussler, who was the President of CBS, and told him who I was and that I was going to work for him some day. Skipping over the chain of command did not do a lot for my collegial work relationships, but Wussler encouraged me. Going to the source worked when I was trying to get the story; it seemed like the logical approach in everything.

I wasn't surprised that the first time I heard that Dad had actually hooked Catfish Hunter for the Yankees was when I read it in the morning newspapers just like everyone else. I had a hunch that Dad would sign Catfish, so when I saw it come across the wire service, I thought I had a line on a human-interest story that no one else had. I knew that to get a big story so soon after making the switch from print to broadcasting was a fast train to my dream of a position at the network. I believed that Dad was loading the bases with another surprise that no one saw coming except me.

So when Dad signed Catfish, I thought I finally had the hook I needed to convince Wussler that I was network-savvy. Dad's deal was the first big free agency signing — it dominated the headlines. My idea was to do an on-air broadcast feature story on what this meant to the future of baseball. I assumed Dad would support me on this story. I offered it to the network. And once I tracked him down, Bob Wussler bit.

Wussler was on a skiing vacation with his family. I think we talked at midnight on a cold, snowy night just before New Year's Eve. I told him about Catfish and asked if this story was big enough to get me to CBS in New York. I remember that he laughed and said I was the only one tenacious enough to find him over the holiday while he was away with his family. He said if I could get my father to go with me and do the interview, then he would clear time during the network's half-time coverage of the Cotton Bowl.

He would fly Dad and me there right away. Wussler and I thought that the father-daughter angle was sweet and soft and exactly what the network wanted for the holiday season. The fact that I would be in New York again, close to Dad, was an added benefit. I needed and wanted his support now as my career was taking off. I was sure Dad would support me on this story. When I called Dad, in my mind I had already packed my bags.

"No!" was all he said.

The silence that followed was deafening, defeating, and devastating. I was speechless. Despite my pleas, Dad denied my request over and over again. I didn't see any reason why he would not work with me on this story. It was already all over the news. I wasn't trying to get details about the contract — I was looking for a feature story told from the inside. I was a sports reporter and I was his daughter. I was dumbfounded that he would not give me what I needed. I saw this as my big break and ticket to a major market as a reporter to be reckoned with in her own right. The way I looked at it, it was a chance for him to encourage me to dream and maybe teach me one of several lifetime lessons that every young woman needs from her Dad. This was a great sports moment for him — a $3.75

million first that validated Dad's position, knowledge, and plan for the New York Yankees.

Instead of a good fish story, we traded unspoken words about the one that got away in our relationship. Dad made more than 500 successful player trades in his career and quite a few less for his daughter.

Sometimes finding someone to tell you that you are right when you feel terribly wronged is too easy. I found it in Bob Wussler. I didn't ask him to write the letter he sent to my father — he took it upon himself to suggest that Dad be more supportive of me. I revered Bob at that time, both for his position and the fact that he stood up for me. The letter broke my dad's silence on this issue.

After reading Bob's letter to my dad questioning his support of his only daughter, Dad called me and said, "Jennie, CBS is just using you to get to me. I will not give in to that kind of pressure and I will not show favoritism to one network. I am not doing the interview."

"Same Auld Lang Syne, Dad. Thanks for your help! Happy New Year, Dad." My bitter tone clashed with the words.

Silence.

I cut the line of communication there. I went back to the NBC network affiliate in Cincinnati and did my job as best I could. I wasn't always good. My voice would go up a few octaves when I got nervous and I had been known to lose my place on the teleprompter, but you couldn't tell me that back then. As far as I was concerned, I had all the qualifications of a major market, on-air sports reporter for CBS.

If Dad was not going to give me my dream, I was going to get it myself. I continued to call Wussler weekly if not daily, repeating that I was going to work for him one day. That day came shortly after I was fired a few months later.

I called Dad to tell him that I had lost my job and that I was coming home to New York. When Dad said he knew the week before that I was going to be fired, I was furious and confused all at once. He said the owner of the station in Cincinnati had written him a letter to tell him that they were letting me go. I felt humiliated, as though everyone knew before me. I took what little pride I had left and headed to New York.

Back in New York I finagled a dinner interview with Bob Wussler. As we ate, Bob motioned toward his ABC network peers who were having dinner at a nearby table. When they noticed that we were looking at them and talking, their conversation got animated and hushed at the same time. The broadcasting executives stopped by our table on the way out of the restaurant.

"Well, hello Bob, aren't you going to introduce us?"

I jumped in and said, "Hi, I'm Jennie Paul, but you can just call me the next Mrs. Wussler," and laughed. I don't even know why I said that.

The men laughed, too, knowing who I was. Everybody in the New York media market knew my dad. "Well if you ever want a job at ABC, Miss….eh…Paul, please call me," said one.

When they left, Bob again advised me to stay at the affiliate where I could grow into the challenge of broadcast work. When I told him that I could not return there because I had been fired, he smiled and said, "Okay, in that case, you are hired."

Two networks were fighting over me — I believed that I had really come far in a short time, all the way to the network without Dad's help. I accepted Bob's offer to be an assistant editor of features for CBS. I sent a dozen roses to my old job in Cincinnati and a note about my new job. I did not have the courage to tell my dad what I had done, but somehow I knew the story would get back to him in much the same way as my dismissal. I never anticipated that the station would miss my joke. My previous employers thought that I was being gracious. They put the roses in the big picture window in the front of the station with a congratulatory note to me so all passersby could see that another one of their own was off to the big time. But the station owner picked up on the barely disguised thorns that I had sent in my farewell. He called my dad. This time, it was to tattle. I heard later that Dad laughed.

Meanwhile, I went about trying to prove to Dad that he was wrong about the reasons Wussler hired me. I worked to get the best interviews and did whatever it took to get the story. I'll never forget how good it felt to get a chance to be the producer for Phyllis George, the former Miss America and a well-liked broadcaster.

She was reporting on the largest fine in the history of women's tennis levied against Margaret Court. Phyllis, the crew and I were in the studio until 4:00 a.m. waiting to catch Ms. Court when she got off a train in Osaka, Japan. The scoop aired on CBS. Phyllis received accolades, and she pulled it off beautifully.

For my part, I was sure that my work on the production and my willingness to make personal sacrifices for a story would show that I could be as serious as my male counterparts. There were not many women in sports media then. With that piece in particular, I felt vindicated. I thought my work spoke for itself and validated my talents as a network-capable producer regardless of who my father was. I felt good.

This time Dad did have advice for me. He called and suggested that I stop working so hard. He said working late was no guarantee of success, and I ought to just try to make it home earlier. I didn't listen. In fact, I was a bit incensed at his double standard in judging my actions compared to his long hours at the office. He stayed up half the night making trades. Why didn't he understand that I was willing to trade a little sleep to be regarded well by my peers and competitors? It was strangely reminiscent of the conversation about winning when he was all about baseball and I was that young equestrian. I was passionate about proving him wrong.

My time in the sun lasted about 15 minutes. Wussler came to me not long after that and asked me to get confidential information on the New York Yankees. In that instant everything Dad had said about CBS came home to me and I felt like Dad was holding my reins in the photo instead of Finley's mule, Charlie–O.

That's how it was with our father-daughter relationship, too. Simple gestures of love were remembered. Small slights fed future one-upmanship struggles that showed up in the oddest places. Why is that?

Dear Dad,

How does that old saying go? Give them a fish or teach them to fish? Dad, if you taught me to fish at the network instead of letting me flounder on my own, I might have eaten for a lifetime instead of feeling like a jackass for a day. I didn't want you to know that you were right, so I never told you about what happened at CBS or why I left.

Dad, I needed to know how to make sense of the disappointing experience and continue to move forward in my career and life. I might have asked you for advice if I had thought you would listen and talk to me. I thought you would just know that I needed you. Instead of trying to protect me by turning your back when I asked you for help, you would have given me a good story of my own to tell.

Dad I am writing you to tell you more than how sad I felt. I want you to know that if you had helped and I failed, I would have been okay. I would have known that you loved me.

You kept our family separated from the Yankees and baseball as much as you could. This "no special treatment philosophy" for me and my brothers pushed us all away from reaching our potential. You went too far, Dad. You did what many of the men of your generation — and perhaps their sons who are the fathers to daughters today — thought was the right thing to do.

I wonder, what did you get out of it when you chose not to support me? If I could have run into your arms, I would have. If you could have welcomed me into your safe protection with words that explained what you were doing, it would have been different between us. I am quite sure that it did not have to take 30 years for me to know that respect is part of love. Today, I know it all made sense to you. But for me, I was left to wonder.

Still, I loved you,

Jennie

5

Billy Martin's Bonus

The blue and white New York Yankees uniform is magical. See it, and you know what you are going to get: sizzle, heat, excitement. You can love them and you can hate them, but you can't ignore them. Before Dad negotiated Billy Martin's first contract to manage the Yankees, he fought George long and hard against giving Martin the job. By the summer of 1975, Dad had transitioned from the more active owner description and status that Steinbrenner had assigned to him to his position as general manager and president. For the time being, George was officially a silent general partner because of his suspension.

My dad was in charge of all the baseball operations, personnel and many of the business decisions. His contract gave him the authority to make player transactions with Steinbrenner's approval, but Dad was far from a rubber stamp. Reporters, owners, and managers regarded him as the true baseball brains of the Yankees. Digging into Steinbrenner's deep pockets, Dad leveraged his relationships on the business side of the game to identify the underdogs and heavy hitters that he needed to restore glory to a team he felt sure would win the World Series again. George wrote the checks.

"If we disagreed on a move," Dad said, "George and I would thrash it out inside the room, not publicly. In most cases, George would go along with my recommendation." Dad liked it that way. The pressure was great, but the rewards of having money and power to do what he wanted helped him reach a pinnacle in his baseball career. In Dad's mind, he was in control. He liked to be in control in all aspects of life, and relationships in particular.

Dad did not want Billy Martin to manage the Yankees. George Steinbrenner did. Up to that point, George had a track record of listening to Dad's counsel on players and managers. As a player, Billy had been volatile. He was a man who was not afraid to open his mouth or get in a fight. Dad knew what Billy was like from personal experience and from encounters relayed to him by players on teams that Dad ran in Cincinnati and Cleveland. Martin had once punched Cubs pitcher Jim Brewer, breaking his cheekbone.

As a manager, the umpires, owners, and players would all be targets for the passionate, unpredictable Martin. Dad's friend, Tommy Lasorda, almost got into a fist fight in 1956 when Billy was a second baseman for the Yankees and Tommy was a pitcher for the Kansas City A's. Billy was a fighter and brought that out in others like a pit bull does when he stares down another dog. According to my dad, Billy was a loser who knew how to win. Knowing what I know, remembering my own experiences being there with Billy, and overhearing parts of the phone conversations when I was at home, I believe the conversation to bring Billy on to the Yankees went something like this:

"We are not going to be number one if Virdon keeps managing the team this way. I didn't buy into this team to be in second place the way it was last year," said Steinbrenner.

"George, Bill (Virdon) is working things out. We are making many changes. He has us in a better place at this point in the season than we were with Houk," said Dad.

"Gabe, Virdon is losing control. He is not good enough to get us where we want to go given the players we have now. We need a strong leader to bring it together. I want Billy Martin in pinstripes. He will pick up the slack, fast."

"Billy Martin is not right for this team, George. You will not be able to work together. He is very different from Virdon. Martin will not go along. Look what happened in Minnesota, Detroit, and Texas after blowups with team owners."

"Gabe, I trust you. I respect you. You know more about baseball than any man I know. But Billy was here when the Yankees were winners. I think Billy has that sense of tradition and fighting spirit we need here. He was a Yankee star when it meant something to be one."

"George, Martin could win, but he's hard to control. He's a fighter. The Copacabana brawl is not his only brush with those who challenge him."

"Gabe, Casey Stengel loved him for what he did to motivate the players around him. He has a fighting spirit. I like that in a man. Burke did, too. He said Billy's desire is to come here again."

Dad ignored the backhanded challenge to his expertise. "George, Casey let him go, and the Twins and the Tigers fired him, too." Dad knew his history well. The owners didn't like Billy. Gabe kept it to the Yankees. "You know what it can be like when Billy, Mickey, Yogi, and Whitey go out."

"Gabe, they are ball players, not saints. It's your call. I know you will make the right decision. I want him. I know that you can handle it," said George.

"George, I can get him. I know what he needs, what he wants. I don't think it is a good idea. He will be trouble. It is already turbulent in that locker room. I don't think he will fit into the mix that we are creating."

"He will make a difference as a motivator."

Although at the beginning Dad was dead set against hiring Billy, he was not about to repeat the mistake that he had made with Judge Roy Hofheinz in this battle for front office control in Houston. Roy and George were cut from the same cloth, Gabe believed. Weighing the choices before him at that stage of his baseball career, Dad committed himself to the idea that owning a number one team he built was more important than being number one in the organization. At the same time, his experience working with George Steinbrenner offered daily reminders that there was a lot that stunk about being number two in a relationship. Somehow, Dad knew how to keep the balance that let him achieve his own dreams.

Working for George Steinbrenner, Dad had to make a whole series of choices that he could tolerate, though not happily. When Virdon's performance started to slip badly, Dad had a harder time fending off George's continual insistence to replace Virdon. He gave in to George on this fight, reserving his power for a more important battle.

"Get rid of Virdon, now Gabe! I didn't want him, but I let him come because you made the deal. I have been patient."

Knowing that Bobby Cox, a name that had come up in earlier conversations as a potential replacement was not up to the job or to George, Gabe finally agreed to pursue Billy.

George wanted Billy and Gabe went about getting him back into the New York Yankees uniform. The public learned of the move during an Old Timer's Day celebration, when Billy stood alongside Joe DiMaggio and Mickey Mantle, cheered by Yankee lovers and Yankee haters.

Bill Virdon walked away from the Yankees without much ceremony, and Billy Martin donned #1 on August 1, 1975. The interesting thing about the number "1" is it can be a high or low value, depending on the situation. Billy Martin would be a high and a low for the New York Yankees, too. Martin would wear the #1 and be fired and rehired by the Yankees a total of five times before his own unhealthy choices would end forever his relationship both with the Yankees on the field and with one who was part of the team but never wore the pinstripes.

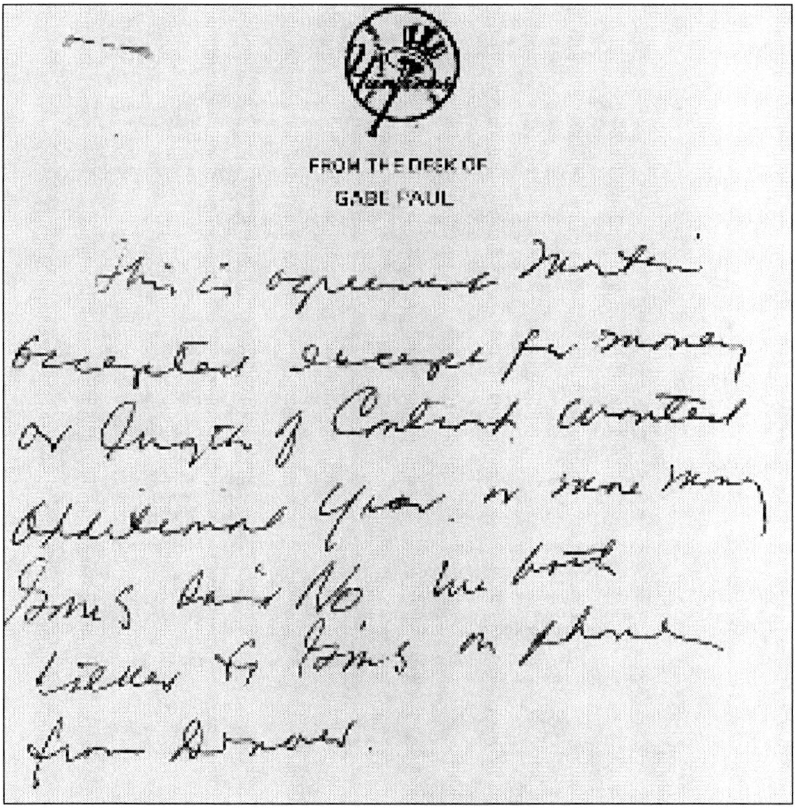

FROM THE DESK OF
GABE PAUL

This is agreement Martin [illegible] except for money or length of contract wanted additional year or more money [illegible]

Gabe's note about agreement with Billy Martin

The following will confirm my understanding with the New York Yankees:

1. I agree to sign a contract to manage the New York Yankees the remainder of the 1975 season and for 1976 for a salary at the rate of Seventy-Two Thousand Dollars ($72,000) per season.

2. I agree that I will be available for consultation on all player acquisition and assignment matters but that final decision in these acquisition and assignment matters will rest with the Yankees' executive management and that I will accept these decisions and not comment on them in a derogatory manner.

3. I agree to cooperate with and accept the organizational procedures and decisions of the player development department and to refrain from interfering in any way with the operation of these departments. However, I will be available for consultation at any time.

4. I will be reimbursed for normal expenses incurred in the performance of my duties for the Yankees but will make no claims for ancillary expenses such as but not limited to personal lodging, country clubs, personal entertainment, etc.

5. I agree to refrain from public criticism of executive management and to adhere to club policies and to personally conduct myself so as to represent the best interests of the New York Yankees.

6. It is understood that I will be judged only by my performance with the players I have at my disposal and the manner in which I represent the best interests of the New York Yankees.

7. All coaches must have the approval of the Yankees' executive management.

8. I will make no commitments to players involving finances and agree that all money matters will be beyond my scope and will be the exclusive right of executive management.

9. Any violation of the above will serve as just cause for termination of this agreement.

By ___Alfred Bill Martin___   Date __8/2/75__
Alfred M. "Billy" Martin

Accepted for New York Yankees

By _____   Date __Aug 5, 1975__

Agreement between Billy Martin and the Yankees

Billy was one of the very few managers who made a difference in the outcome of a game, a season, and the way a team blended…or didn't. Like him or not, the team won a lot more games when Billy was in charge than when someone else was running the Yankees.

Dad's diary contained a note that was in stark contrast to the heated discussions leading up to signing Billy. George found ways to make his views about the Yankees very clear to Gabe, letting my dad know that he was in it to win it. Dad was an important key to that combination, and he knew George understood it. Frankly, he was surprised that George admitted it in a letter he left behind for Dad:

Note to Gabe from George Steinbrenner, 8/3/1975

Managing the last half of the 1975 season, Billy is credited with adding 30 wins and 26 losses to the Yankees regular season record. The Yankees finished the season in third place with a record of 83-77, just 12 games behind the pennant-winning Boston Red Sox, and four games ahead of the Indians that Dad had left behind two years before. Dad's year of trades and team building continued while Billy managed the team with a sure hand. Catfish Hunter went 23-14 in a career-best 328 innings in 1975, finishing second behind Jim Palmer in the American League Cy Young Award voting after winning the award the year before. Martin's record for the games he managed that year was a .536 compared to Virdon's .510, which vindicated George and created a baseball love-hate triangle among George, Billy, and Dad. The Yankees were a contender again, but not a champion yet. The three wanted more — they could almost taste the victory.

Dad's prediction about the inability of George and Billy to work together and with others proved to be correct. Gabe became the antacid in that relationship, and he found a way to bring out each man's strengths while reducing the corrosiveness of their weaknesses.

George still had to prove he was number one, even though Billy wore that number on the field, and so the war of wills began. It was a pattern that Billy had experienced in many other places. That attitude would cost him a few jobs. He was fired seven times as a manager, but he is most famous for his five stints with the Yankees.

Billy's first time with the Yankees was notable because Billy and George had my dad as a buffer, a peacemaker to stand between them. Dad wrote in his diary about a trait that I knew well from my own experiences. "Billy is not a man who is known for keeping his mouth shut." No argument, there.

Billy Martin was not gracious. He didn't give George points for hiring him. Rather, he was disgusted that George had appointed himself an instant expert. Billy felt George was just a sports fan who happened to be the general partner of a great team. Every day when George made a suggestion or a criticism, it would get under Billy's skin. George and Billy got into it a few times. They fought behind closed doors and they fought in the newspapers, trading barbs, comments, and headlines on the sports pages and programs across America. Billy and George were at each other's throats so often that their relationship was spoofed on late-night comedy and in beer commercials.

Gabe Paul and Billy Martin

Billy Martin respected my dad for what he knew, and he enjoyed the challenge of working with the many different player personalities and dynamics that Gabe created with his complex trades. But Billy did not appreciate Steinbrenner's power challenges to his management decisions, nor did he like the way George tried to buddy up with the players. Dad and Billy were in close agreement on this one, and the players enjoyed the locker room game as much as the one on the field. George wanted to be a man among the players, but Dad understood that a clear separation had to be kept between management and personal attachment at the player level. While he and George sparred on this point on many occasions, Dad loved and respected the players, as they did him.

had to be kept between management and personal attachment at the player level. While he and George sparred on this point on many occasions, Dad loved and respected the players, as they did him.

The line of people who wanted to have a relationship with my dad and his new manager Billy Martin was very long. I was one of those people, fighting to get closer to both men for different reasons. The choices that a girl makes when her father is absent at crucial times are not unlike the decisions a team manager must make. Questions like who to cut and who to keep are always on your mind. You don't want holes in your line-up and you want to be ready if one of your starters gets hurt or can't play.

Dads that don't show up when their daughters need them raise girls with an ache and a hole in their heart. As the pangs from the void in our father-daughter relationship got worse, I looked for Dad in all the wrong places. I began to develop an unhealthy appetite for men who were not good for me. They had Dad's undesirable characteristics and none of his good. They were emotionally unavailable; they were fillers. One of them was Billy Martin. Yes, I was Billy Martin's girlfriend for a time. If Dad had ever found out, they would have challenged each other on much more than tactics.

I remember Billy Martin as far back as 1960 when he was with the Cincinnati team. It was August 4th, my 9th birthday, and even then I was watching the game for excitement. Billy got in a fight that day. I don't remember why he charged the pitcher's mound, but it fed my feisty spirit the way it makes hockey fans get excited when they see a fight break out on the ice. I am always looking for that something special on my birthday to mask some of the sadness when I cannot let go of the idea that something is missing. Casey and I found it in Billy that day and many times after that.

Casey Stengel loved Billy for the fire he could start under the butts and feet of all the other players when he was a World Series caliber player. At 24, I loved Billy for this reason and more. I liked how Billy went after the media when they asked him the same question too many times or pushed him too far, challenging his decisions in the game and his behavior after the lights on the field went out. Billy was the epitome of life. His eyes were full of sparkle and to me, he seemed like he walked ten feet off the ground.

He was never still. He bounced like Tigger. He stopped just long enough to take you on a ride with him if you were willing. He was magnetic and made people laugh. He loved girls. He was smart and witty. He was full of surprises on and off the field. Dad used to say on a regular basis that Billy was a "skirt chaser." "Anything in skirts," Dad would say. I put on a skirt. Dad was right. Nothing passed by Billy in the game or in a short dress. I guess I fit the bill.

In 1976, the New York Baseball Writers' Association honored Dad with the Bill Slocum award at their annual dinner for long and meritorious service to baseball. The dinner was by invitation only and women were excluded; even women sportswriters weren't granted an exception. I was incensed and determined to get inside the all-male sanctum and find out what was so special. I snuck in with Mom, yes, Mom, the prim and proper beauty queen. The plan worked until we ran into Billy Martin and Mickey Mantle.

I thought Billy was going to expose us. His eyes narrowed as he asked, "Where are you two going?"

Was Billy being coy? I didn't know for sure. Figuring I had nothing to lose, I just parroted his question with a flirty tone, "Where are you going?"

Billy laughed. Zeroing in on my brazenness and mindful of Mom's presence, he dropped his business-like face and decided to play along. "The same place you're going," he said.

Mickey laughed. He came too.

We slipped into the balcony of the theatre and listened from a vantage point few had. That's the way it was in my relationship with Billy Martin. Hidden from the rest, we heard the planned presentations and the remarks that did not get published. That gave us a lot to laugh at and talk about that night.

I had given Dick Young, a well-known New York sportswriter and the Master of Ceremonies for that event, a heartfelt letter honoring my Dad and our relationship. I asked him to read it at the dinner. In the letter, I spoke of my father's accomplishments, and then I finished it with, "I love you Dad." It was full of genuine respect and admiration and everyone in the audience who had a daughter or knew someone who had a daughter could have related. It was a beautiful letter stating that I knew when he was pained and I had his back. I waited in the balcony, listening. I couldn't wait to see the look on his face. Dick Young never read it.

It might have been a bit emotional for a bunch of men to hear, but it would have been the highlight of my evening. Maybe he gave it to Dad. I don't know. My guess was that he did. I went home, and I waited to see if Dad would mention anything about it. Dad was silent and I felt let down.

I certainly wasn't going to bring it up. I told my younger brother Henry, whom I had flown in for the occasion to surprise Dad, that I was going out. As soon as Mom and Dad closed the door, I kissed my almost grownup baby brother and told him I was going to PJ Clarke's to meet Billy and Mickey. When I snuck out of the condo we had at 69th and 3rd that night, I told Henry I would only be gone for a short while.

I could not wait to meet Billy, sure that he would be the warmth I needed that night. I took a cab down to 55th to Billy's favorite sports hangout where we sat close together, holding hands under the table.

I was aching from Dad not saying anything about the letter. It had taken a lot of time to find the right words to tell him how important he was to me. I wanted to tell Billy, and believed that Billy would comfort me.

My drink of choice, a vodka martini with lots of olives, multiplied at the table. There were ten of them when I lost count. Billy and I were deep in conversation as people kept buying drinks and sending them to our table. One drink I was okay. Two I was high. After three, I felt sick. I tried to pace myself, wanting to be with Billy and do what he did. At one point, about 3:00 a.m. I thought of my brother waiting up for me. Thinking I should check in with him, I went back to the condo.

I stumbled down the hall and rode up in the elevator with an elevator man which was just as well since I couldn't have found the right floor on my own. I fiddled with my key and opened the door. A few steps inside I knocked over a lamp and started giggling. Henry was sleeping on the couch in the living room and was blearily happy to see me. I told him that I just wanted to let him know that I was okay.

I turned around and headed back to PJ Clarke's to be with Billy. Fueled by several too many vodka martinis I was feeling brave. Dad and Mom were asleep and I was riding in a limo. But halfway there I had to tell the limo driver to pull over. There, in the middle of the fashionable east side of Manhattan on my way to see Billy Martin and Mickey Mantle, I puked out the door of an elegant stretch limo. It was not one of my better moments.

We closed PJ Clarke's that night. The next day, Billy and I picked up where we left off. I went to his hotel and when Billy started drinking, I tried to keep up with him, drinking to numb my feelings. Billy Martin helped me get over the hurt of that unread letter. When I needed him, he was there. I never had to impress him. Billy liked me and accepted me as I was. It was the first of many late nights and long talks between me and Billy Martin.

Anyone who knows me knows I can't drink much. The alcohol deadened the pain of my father's lack of connection with me very quickly. "Am I that different than other women?" I asked Billy during one of our many late night talks.

After listening for a while, Billy asked, "Jennie, what is it about your Dad that bugs you so much? You talk like you love him in one breath and then you act like you hate him in the next."

"I don't know Billy. Maybe it's the way he treats me when I am working on a story. Maybe it's the fact that he is always trying to get me to date his boring business associates instead of someone like you. Dad would not like it if he knew about us, Billy."

"Your Dad doesn't know about us. And if he did, if it bothered him, he'd do something about it…that is how your Dad is." Billy grinned.

"Did I tell you what he did when I showed up at the stadium in my Charles Jourdan $235 purple cowboy boots? Dad hated them."

"I would have liked those boots," Billy grinned.

"He looked at the boots and then Dad said he didn't like me. He said it in front of all his friends. That really hurt me. They were just boots. I thought they were great but his friends made a big deal out of it. It just made me realize how much I don't want to live some boring life, giving up what I like based on someone else's opinion. Mom gave up everything for Dad's passion."

"Talk to him, Jennie. I always find your Dad easy to talk to. Now, George he is another story. He's as mulish as I am. George and I don't get anywhere when we talk. Your dad is different," Billy went on.

"Talk to Dad? Are you kidding? Every time I think I want to sit down and tell him how I feel, I can't. I feel like somehow it's my fault that we cannot find the words. I don't feel loved, and I know he doesn't like me."

"Jennie, he doesn't like me either, but I know he loves what I do for him. Moreover, I love what he does for me. He challenges me to be me. I bet your Dad loves you the same way. That's enough. It's more than I got from my dad and mom put together."

"I want my dad to love me and like me," I said. "Billy, I want the same patience and communication that Dad has with you."

"Jennie, c'mere," Billy said, grabbing me with one hand and a bottle with the other.

Then Billy kissed me, touched me, and scooped me up in his arms for a night neither of us would remember in any great detail. The sex was not that good, even though I wanted it to be. Maybe Billy thought it was. Men remember things differently when they don't remember anything at all. That is the way it always is when alcohol comes to bed with you and your man.

Billy and I started seeing each other more after that night. Whenever I looked to Dad for validation or assurance that I was doing the right thing, he would deliver one of his famous Paulisms. "Look on the sunny side of the street..." Whatever message I was supposed to get from that fell short of its target. It was hard for me to talk to him. But when I was with Billy Martin, I could pretend that I was not full of fear. Billy and I touched each other, finding a connection in the emptiness that few suspected dominated us both. I continued meeting him, mostly in hotels. Our on-again, off-again, sometimes relationship was temporarily comforting. When we were together I didn't dwell on reasoning because I knew where the night was heading — satisfying Billy's insatiable need for shallow sex. I accepted sex in place of love and it always left me feeling empty and hungry for real love.

Billy Martin was not a healthy choice for a relationship, but in my early twenties, he was exactly what I wanted. I did not want to be married, and clearly neither did Billy, considering the many women he loved and let go and on again off again, married. I believed I loved Billy Martin. He was whimsical and daring. I got a thrill from walking on the edge with him. Billy was so smart and he knew the game of baseball better than most. He loved my dad, and I think Dad loved him too, even though Dad didn't really like him and may even have hated him at the same time. No wonder I went out and drank with Billy. In my trysts with Billy I was laced with guilt that Dad would not approve. Maybe I was testing Dad. I wondered, if he knew, would he still love me?

While Dad was wheeling and dealing, my life was reeling. I had all these questions and feelings that I didn't know what to do with when it came to Billy Martin and Dad. I just could not bring myself to ask my dad for advice on relationships, even though he clearly was an expert. A 59-year marriage and the men of baseball who frequented our living room were testament to what he knew about relationships, baseball and the commitments that matter most in life. Thirty years later, I know it would have been better if we had had a sincere conversation about these values. I know what I would say now.

Dear Dad,

Mom said you knew about Billy and me, but you chose not to say anything to me. It must have killed you the way I defied your need to control me, when I choose Billy Martin instead of the safer alternatives that you offered. You pushed so hard for me to be with men who were conservative and restrained, and yet you said nothing about the man who was so clearly their opposite. You knew the dark side of your manager, whereas I saw only the excitement.

If Billy Martin was wrong for me, the men you introduced me to were no better because they would have consumed my sense of self. I saw the one love you had with

Mom, sustaining your 59-year union. You two were so in love when you married — the Florida Orange Queen at 17 and you at 29. You and Mom worked through having five kids, little money, career choices/demands, and ill health. There had to be more to your relationship than longevity. What was it?

As much as I did not want you to save me from Billy, I wanted you to rescue me from a pattern of running away from the conversation that I could have initiated as easily as you might have if only one of us said what no one said.

I could have asked you what you thought of the letter I gave to Dick. I could have asked you to encourage me and challenge me instead of trying to hold me back or under your thumb. I could have asked you to say what you were thinking about my life choices with a voice of unconditional love instead of being so critical. I could have pushed harder for an in depth conversation on how to protect my self-interests without forsaking love or my pioneering spirit.

The fact is that I did not ask you these direct questions. It would have been better if I did. It was easier to just go to Billy. I thought he had all these answers.

Today as I look back and think about how much I love you still today, Dad, I wonder why we avoided the emotion between us, and shared it so openly with others.

I miss you, Dad.

Jennie

6
Independence Day

It was 1976 and America was celebrating two hundred years of independence. In New York the fireworks were not limited to that spectacular display viewed from Battery Park. The New York Yankees and Gabe Paul were celebrating, too. It had been just a few years since Dad's ownership group acquired the team from CBS. Dad was very much in charge. George's money and frequent cash calls to the investors made Dad's empire-building possible.

With the freedom to make trades and sign players without regard to the cost, Dad pulled off a series of brilliant deals. He used his independence from George's control to trade for something far more valuable than a brass ring: Dad had his eye on a World Series championship ring. He put everything in place for what would prove to be a history-changing season.

Then Bowie Kuhn lifted George's suspension early, citing financial hardship on the team from the delayed renovations to Yankee Stadium, which forced the team to play at Shea Stadium longer than planned. George Steinbrenner was back and happy again to be a visible part of the winning team that Dad was building. But as much as George wanted to win, he desired control more. The fighting started soon after George came back from his suspension.

Besides Dad and George, there was another who saw and heard all the internal fireworks. Pearl Davis told me:

Gabe at his desk in Shea Stadium

They could have worked it out, if they had more respect for each other, but that's not how it happened. Like Gabe, I knew every player and every staff person. I ran things as secretary to the president of the New York Yankees. It was my stadium, and I felt like it was as much my team as did Gabe and George. George began a series of moves that would push many of the owners and players around one minute and then in the next, try to be a buddy. Players, coaches, sportswriters, and even the fans saw this side of him. The hard-to-take polices originated with George. He left the tough stuff to Gabe to carry out, and did not defend your dad when people were unhappy about the changes to the team. As the years went by, I saw him disrespect Gabe and many others. George had a temper. I heard him. It is no secret now, but back then we did not know exactly what to make of him. I think Gabe was surprised, too. He took a lot from Mr. Steinbrenner. Gabe had a hard time with the way George operated, but he stayed silent about many things.

One day, I went into Mr. Paul's office after he and Mr. Steinbrenner had one of those brain-bashing matches. Mr. Steinbrenner stormed out as though everything that needed to be said had been said. Mr. Paul was upset, and yet he did not want to talk about it or draft a memo on the meeting as he had on so many previous occasions after one of George's tirades. Instead, Mr. Paul talked about baseball and the fact that he was recording his memories. I was not sure what he wanted me to do at that moment, and so I just sat there and listened. There were many times, he said, "I remember...and remember...and remember..." as he reflected on the long hours and years with the Yankees and the other teams that had been his stepping stones to New York.

The words that came from Mr. Paul were the kind that come from a person's gut when they are hurting. He mumbled about working long hours, being too strict and distant — just not being with his family as much as he would like.

Mr. Paul said, "I have been selfish in some ways and I know now that you cannot be selfish and happy at the same time. I have not handled the love part of life very well and I've hurt those who tried. I love to be loved." It was a moment of vulnerability I had not seen in all the years that I worked for him. "I hide it from those close to me, especially, my beautiful, gutsy Jennie. She should have been a boy," he said lovingly with a smile tugging at the corners of his face. He treasured you so very dearly, and I felt his pain as he spoke.

I felt the presence of the wonderful Savior's love and my own at that moment. Our religions might have been different, my boss' and mine, but our hearts brought us together in the name of the God we loved and served. You see: Lazarus had Jesus, Joshua had Moses, Timothy had Paul, Esther had Mordecai, and Gabe had me, the gal from Harlem, Pearline B. Davis.

My moment of introspection and protectiveness came to an end quickly, when suddenly, Mr. Paul signaled I should take dictation and said, "And so to my Jennie I leave behind this message…

"I said a prayer for you today — you may not have known that I was thinking of you at this moment. I said a prayer for you today asking for your forgiveness, your well-being, your good health, abundant love for all of your tomorrows, your peace of mind, your strength of spirit and especially your love for me. The greatest gift I can give to you now is my prayers and I gladly do so knowing that the Lord, whom I have come to know is active in your heart and mine forever.

"I said a prayer to the Lord today and gave thanks to Him who gave me my wonderful wife Mary, my wonderful children, Gabe Jr., Warren, Henry, Michael, and you Jennie. I said a prayer for myself today that the love present in me will open the gates of your heart and let me in. I live only in the moment now and realize that my journey is my destination. I now know that you will never know love until you surrender to it. I now surrender ALL, right now! A long life may not be good enough but a good life is certainly long enough."

He stopped talking. He closed his eyes, without finishing the letter. I knew it was time for me to go; I took my pad and went back to my desk.

> The next day, Gabe Paul was gone from Yankee Stadium and our front office. He quit. He went home to be with his family.

How does a man, so close to reaching his lifelong dream, simply walk away? For Dad, it would not be the first time he would quit, nor the last. When Dad walked away from George Steinbrenner that day it was just a few months before opening day in 1976. He left his team when they needed him most, and returned to his home in Florida where we needed him more.

George understood that Dad loved baseball and appreciated the players, the coaches, and the game behind the scenes. He was all baseball, and he was all business. As much as Steinbrenner hated the idea of relying on a man of such strength and knowledge, George knew he needed Dad. Whatever else he did, George became a success because he surrounded himself with people who were good at their jobs. George went to Florida to entice Dad to come back to New York.

Steinbrenner promised my dad more money, power, freedom, and control. George again agreed to operate with a hands-off policy, leaving the running of the team to Billy and the operations to Gabe. Déjà vu! Like that day in the Pewter Mug, the offer was almost irresistible. Dad wanted to believe that he got what he asked for, and yet he consulted his peer and friend Howard Cosell before answering George.

I had a chance to get to know Howard and knew that he had the ability to play or say what George wanted, and what Dad wanted. In fact, I think he egged them on at several junctures. Then in my early twenties, I thought I was the only one who could see that Howard played both sides of the fence. To me it looked like Howard was using Dad. To Dad, Howard was a friend and an accomplished professional who had similarly overcome some of the prejudices that existed against people of the Jewish faith. Dad wanted so much to be an owner of a winner, and Howard encouraged him to believe in George if he could and the New York Yankees if he would. Leaving his family to return with George to the Yankees in exchange for an irresistible offer to have his dream would prove to be a recurring theme in his life, and a foreshadowing of many such times when he would walk away from me.

Gabe Paul with Howard Cosell and Steve O'Neill

Reality set in quickly. What George's deal meant for Dad was more responsibility than many of the baseball executives of other teams. With the Yankees, Dad had the budget and the team most general managers or presidents would kill for, and the pressure that makes you wonder why anyone would want to take the job in the first place — unless of course it is first place that you covet. Gabe's resignation and return were kept out of the press and known to only a few. Meanwhile, George would take the credit for Gabe's work and quickly forget his promise to let Billy manage the Martin way.

New York Yankees

Office Communication

to: Gabe Paul

from: G. M. S. III

RE: MEETING 2/12/76

DATE: February 13, 1976

As we discussed, Gabe, I want to set down herewith the things we spoke about yesterday so that there are no misunderstandings on either of our parts and so that we can get about the business which is paramount to both of us -- the building of the Yankees.

First, let me say that regarding the resignation which you submitted a week ago for my acceptance without dwelling on it, I think I made my feelings clear. It was something I could not understand or accept. It would not have been fair to you. So, we will put that behind us.

Secondly, I know that the pressures of the past two years have been great, what with my suspension, the new stadium, player problems, and our collapse in '75. I also know that your career spans some 45 years in baseball, and I do not think you or I want that career to end with any problem to your health from the pressures whatever.

In view of all the things we talked about yesterday, here then is what I feel we arrived at:

1. You will remain as President of the Yankees and will be paid $50,000 per year. The new agreement will run until January 15, 1978, just as the other agreement. It would be my suggestion that at that time we look at this again because you may feel you do not wish to continue past that point.

2. You will reside in Tampa, Florida, and in your capacity as President you will work directly with me as General Partner. If you would like, Gabe, you could have an office in with us in Tampa. I think that would be really a good set up.

3. Your workload and schedule will be your own responsibility to set up as you see fit to carry out properly your areas of responsibility.

Memo to Gabe Paul from George Steinbrenner — page 1 of 4

MEMO TO: Gabe Paul
Page 2
February 13, 1976

Regarding those areas of responsibility, I see them basically as follows:

1. To attend all League and baseball meetings where we
    feel our attendance is necessary. It may very well
    be that I will not attend many of the meetings, and
    then if we felt it necessary to have someone there,
    you would attend alone.

2. To be responsible for all trades with the other
    clubs subject to the General Partner's approval --
    and we have never had any problems there. This
    will naturally necessitate travel to view our own
    team as well as other teams.

3. To zero in on our farm system -- not necessarily
    the drafting of players, but to see that the
    entire system is organized and functioning the
    way it should, but has not. To see that we·
    get the material we draft to the Big Leagues.
    This is going to be tough because we are in such
    bad shape -- but if we are to build this thing,
    we must do a complete evaluation and reorganiza-
    tion on the farm system. We have and are spending
    far too much for the results we have gotten!

4. The scouting system -- you know my feelings on
    this -- I intend to make this a main area of
    my involvement in the next several years, and
    I will look to you for counsel in this area
    also.

5. You will attend the full spring training without
    interruption of your baseball duties, unless it
    is absolutely necessary in my opinion due to the
    opening of the new stadium where some area might
    pop up which Cedric is not familiar with.

    Frankly, I want your talents utilized where they
    can do us the most good; that is evaluating per-
    sonnel and consummating trades. No one can argue
    that you have probably made the greatest trades
    in the history of the game. We're just a bit
    shy of what we need in my opinion. A couple of
    good trades could do it for us this year, and

Memo to Gabe Paul from George Steinbrenner — page 2 of 4

MEMO TO: Gabe Paul
Page 3
February 13, 1976

then we have to think about the future. I don't
want your mind muddled with a lot of other decision-
making when we get ready to decide what and who we
want to go after and what we can afford to give.

6. You and I will sit with Cedric next week. He will
become Vice President - Operations with full
responsibility for the new stadium; recognizing,
of course, that there are some areas that will
require your and my attention to bring to a head.
These areas I wish you would concentrate on <u>very</u>
<u>hard</u> for the next few weeks to bring them to a
point where we know whether or not we have a problem, and if we do, to get them resolved or at
least in the process toward final resolution.
Those I know of now are:

   a. The $90,000 plus air-conditioning matter
     with Canco.

   b. The matter of the structural and design
     changes made for the Conrac scoreboard.

   c. The matter of the two large luxury suites.

   d. The selling of advertising space on the
     scoreboard.

   e. The request by WPIX for us to participate
     in some of their costs -- which we will
     not do.

   f. The lack lustre performance of our ticket
     salesmen in the area of "new" season seat
     sales.

7. I will be working closely with the finance people
and, of course, may need your counsel there also.

In summation, Gabe, let me try to capsulize if I can. I see our
working relationship being closer than ever before. This may
please you; it may not -- but I think when this ball club was
going best, we were working closest.

You will be the guy who will be looked to for our personnel moves --
what we need, where we get it, and you will consummate our deals. This

Memo to Gabe Paul from George Steinbrenner — page 3 of 4

MEMO TO: Gabe Paul
Page 4
February 13, 1976

area will be one of the two primary areas you will be involved in.

The other area will be the farm system -- the guts of our operation.
It is terrible and we look to you to revamp, restructure, or whatever.
Young Nugent, if he's as good as you say, can learn a lot from you
and we should groom him within the system we want.

You know we both agree we've got too many clubs, and we have to work
to change that; but more immediate is the plain and simple fact that
"our capital invested" is not producing "income" and when that happens
in a business, the business goes bankrupt.

You'll have to start from the bottom -- from the crummy uniforms on up.
We just have to make it function the way it should.

Now in concentrating on these areas, I realize travel will be involved,
and I think we reached an understanding about expenses. I have adjusted
the budget upward from $12,000 to $18,000, and as you and I discussed, if
it takes more, well then, I will get it for you; but this I felt was a
reasonable guideline without the heavy New York T & E. We had to have
some point for the budget.

On the other areas we are working so hard to bring in line like phone
costs, etc. We have a WATS line at Tampa which you would have in your
office also, and I am sure that we'll be able to live with our cuts
there. For one thing, we won't be having to call each other long
distance so much.

Again, Gabe, you will set your own schedule. I think I know you well
enough to know that it will be whatever it takes to get the job done.
I look forward to being able to bounce ideas back and forth regularly
across the desk and not 1,000 miles apart with a hundred intermediaries.
I know that this has caused many of our problems in the past year. However, I also want you and Mary to be able to relax a little, play some
golf and have a "life-style" a little more pleasant than it has been
the past few years.

/lr

Memo to Gabe Paul from George Steinbrenner — page 4 of 4

Gabe was fair to all the reporters covering the Yankees, but
he had a special definition of fair reserved for Howard Cosell,

a powerful man who was well known for his sharp mind and sharper tongue. His play-by-play announcing and color commentary made covering sports as newsworthy as the outcome of the contest itself. A controversial trendsetter in sports journalism, this man was very influential with Dad. Gabe had nearly let this dream of being a winner slip through his fingers. Some who knew what happened speculated that Dad returned to New York at Steinbrenner's urging, and it was true. But without Cosell's strong validation of whatever rationalization he offered, Dad might have stayed in Florida and missed his ride from great potential to the first of three pennants and two gold championship rings — one of which would become the New York Yankees pendant I wear today.

Dad and Howard had begun their friendship years before, and it became deeper when Gabe bought and ran the Yankees. Dad liked Cosell's edginess in the same way that he liked it in Billy Martin. Both men were smart and faithful to their principles as was Gabe. Bound by history and a deep knowledge of the game of baseball at its most tactical level, Dad and Howard had a bond unlike any other.

Howard Cosell challenged Gabe Paul intellectually and emotionally, although only in sports and religion. Cosell was not afraid to say what was on his mind, and in fact dead air space was rarely a problem when he was doing the color commentary, analysis and broadcast for the Muhammad Ali (Cassius Clay) fights and both "Monday Night Football" and baseball. Was Howard's motivation for his friendship with Dad less than completely honorable? In my view, Howard's insider view of baseball would not have been so complete without Dad's knowledge. Howard saw Dad's absence from the Yankees as a big negative, perhaps because he cared for Dad's dreams, and perhaps because he would lose his source of information and special access to the Yankees. If Howard was using him, Dad didn't seem to mind. Sports fans knew who Howard

Cosell was, and both he and Dad were recognized frequently by Yankee fans and Yankee haters alike when they walked to their favorite diner. They were principled men with strengths and weaknesses, and Dad's reserve offset Howard's sometimes strident voice. It was certainly not a one-sided relationship. To be on Cosell's good side meant favorable reporting and information on players and teams that other general managers might not have been privy to.

Likewise, Gabe's affinity for Billy was not limited to what he could do on a baseball field, and as much as Billy was like Howard in terms of his intelligence and understanding of the game, Dad liked him for his unique perspective on playing the game. Both Billy and Howard were winners in their careers with and without Dad, and he respected them for that. Dad allowed them to be weak at times because he valued them when they were strong. Perhaps he saw some of his weaknesses in them and found solace in his times of superiority.

By the end of 1976, Billy Martin managed Gabe's and George's team right into pennant contention. Catfish Hunter's 17-15 record in 1976 helped push the Yankees into the World Series. Dad had built a formidable ball club with the likes of Ken Holtzman, Doyle Alexander, Ken Brett, Willie Randolph, Dock Ellis, Lou Piniella, Ed Figueroa, Mickey Rivers, Oscar Gamble, Chris Chambliss, Roy White, Fritz Peterson, Elston Howard, Graig Nettles, Thurman Munson, Ron Guidry, Sandy Alomar, and Fran Healy.

The New York Yankees would be facing Dad's old team in the World Series. From a distance, Dad watched the Cincinnati team he built and left behind win victories for which he laid the foundation. The fact that the names on the Reds rosters were different in 1976 did little to diminish Dad's appetite to eat his alma mater for lunch.

Winning the American League pennant restored the fans' faith in the Yankees who had fallen short every season for the last 12 years. Dad's next challenge was the World Series where he would face the Cincinnati Reds. The last time the Yankees and the Reds had met in the post-season championship was 1961. That time, the Yankees took home the championship; Gabe Paul, Billy Martin, and George Steinbrenner each hungered for history to be repeated. But the bicentennial fireworks ended for the Yankees as the Reds swept in four games and took home the World Series championship ring in 1976.

Although his Yankees lost the series that year, the history-making pennant win invigorated Yankees players, fans, and owners alike. Gabe would let the Reds have the last word this season.

While the battle for ultimate control between Dad, George and Billy played out during the 1976 season, I was making my own moves as a sports broadcaster, consistently pitching stories that were getting picked up by Metromedia, Warner Brothers, and HBO.

Steve Ross, from Warner Brothers Communications, hired me to redo a piece on the international star Pelé's arrival on the New York Cosmos soccer team, and the result was good enough to get me more feature-reporting jobs including the last interview given by Mrs. Babe Ruth before she died.

I did a story on the new head football coach at Gallaudet University, whose hearing-impaired football team was competing with and winning against hearing teams. The story showed how these players communicated with one another using sign language. To connect with the audience, I included a sign language interpreter on the screen, which was not then widely done. The piece aired on NBC's "GrandStand" with Bryant Gumble, and the network submitted my report on its sports Emmy reel. None of my stories were about the Yankees, Dad, or what he was doing with his team. I was enjoying my independence from the pressure of being Gabe Paul's daughter. Instead of feeling like I was being used to get information from my dad about his team, I was starting to get recognized for my own approach to feature reporting. In 1976, I felt as though I was on top of my game, just like any other 25-year-old woman in step with the times, happy to be free of her father's control. HBO hired me to do 11 feature stories around the country, and so I left New York, the Yankees, Dad, and Billy Martin.

Dad's 1976 season ended about the same time as my stint with HBO. When that contract ended I went back to Florida to recover in more ways than one. Despite my independence and hard work, my life was once again in a downward spiral. Unknown to my family, I was dealing with the emotional and physical trauma of an abortion. (No, it wasn't Billy's baby.) My family knew I was between jobs and sad, but I could not tell them there was more to my depression than losing yet another job that I loved.

When Howard Cosell and the other sportscasters interviewed my dad and George Steinbrenner after the Yankees lost the series, each had a very different perspective on why the Yankees had lost the championship. Dad was a man of few words. He talked about the players and about his manager. George claimed most of the credit for the team's performance while sidestepping the issue of the loss.

Watching that interview, I felt intense empathy for my dad. Owning a World Series winner was his dream, and it had just been denied him by the very team that he once owned. I knew how he felt. When they cut to a clip of Billy Martin arguing with an umpire about a call that went against him, I could hardly watch for the pain it caused. I wanted to be with Dad and with Billy. But before I could start to pack my bags, Dad was back home in Florida with me and Mom.

With time I started to feel better, yet when I told my dad that I wanted to get back into sports reporting in New York, he was none too supportive. But when I told him that I had applied to be an airline flight attendant, and did not get a job offer despite a great interview, that was something he could fix. To him, flying with an airline was good work for a single woman. He made a few calls, including one to George Steinbrenner.

I'll never know which of these men was my hero that day, but TWA hired me a few weeks later and based me at their International Hub in Boston. Flying around the world meant I was also where many of the best sports stories happened. I pitched Metromedia Channel 5 on feature stories on basketball in Italy, tennis in France and at Wimbledon, and the Maccabiah Games (the "Jewish Olympics") in Israel.

Jennie on the radio

Once again I was flying high. I was close to many of the most popular athletes, coaches, and sports journalists. My dad and

Billy Martin were close, and yet I was as far away from them as I wanted to be. I was back in sports, pitching stories and getting airtime in New York, Los Angeles, Kansas City, and Boston. My hunger for broadcasting sports was insatiable, and the fact that flight attendants did not fly every week meant I had downtime to do something about it.

With my usual audacity, I pitched the concept for a weekly sports trivia show to WITS, the Red Sox's 50,000-watt station in Boston. I got it, becoming the first woman in the country to do a show like that. My radio show was popular, and I was always looking for something to keep the audience coming back. When my research for the show turned up a surprising statistic about athletes who died young, it moved me. I looked for a local angle.

I found it in Harry Agganis, a great football and baseball player who had died suddenly in 1955. Boston Red Sox owner Tom Yawkey had signed Agganis to his team in 1952 and was so inspired by the young athlete that he co-founded a foundation along with the (Lynn, MA) Daily Item newspaper, Harold O. Zimman, and the Boston Red Sox organization. Through the Harry Agganis Foundation some $1.3 million has been awarded for college scholarships to student/athletes in Eastern Massachusetts. The Agganis Arena at Boston University is named in his honor.

Broadcasting human-interest sports stories had become my passion. My story was full of human interest, trivia, and numbers, and the connection to the headlines of the day made it ripe for a weekend's radio broadcast. The audience loved it, and I decided to do an expanded human-interest feature for my submission to New York Channel 5's "Sunday Sports Extra" the following week. I did the report while I walked around a field where Harry played at Boston University, drawing the audience in, creating a sense of being there. To add more relevance to my New York audience, I talked about Aggannis' incredible accomplishments in sports, zeroing in on a game between the Red Sox and the Yankees.

Howard Cosell, Nori Shea, Mary Paul, Emmy Cosell, Bill Shea

I was very proud of that story. It was the same as all my other features in its human-interest appeal, and yet it turned out quite a bit differently than I expected when I started to put the story together. When it aired, I was at my parents' apartment in New York. Dad was there watching with me along with Howard Cosell who happened to be visiting that day. Among the many things Dad and Howard shared were a Jewish heritage, a love for baseball, and daughters who aspired to careers that ran parallel to their fathers'. Since my fans in Boston and my producer in New York had loved the story, I was anticipating what I was sure would be the validation from my dad that I had wanted for so many years. If others liked it, I reasoned, Dad would recognize how far I had come since my first on-air assignment back in Cincinnati. I was certain he would be proud of me.

When the piece ended, Dad was silent.

Howard spoke first. That is when I found out that no one was safe from Howard Cosell, not even his dearest friend's daughter.

"Jennie that is the worst piece of reporting I have ever seen! Why would you do a report for a local New York station while walking around a stadium in Boston and talking about one of their dead players? If you think that this is sports reporting, you might as well just get out of broadcasting. Honestly, Jennie that is a disgrace. You want to know sports reporting, look at the way my daughter Hilary covers the news. She does it the right way"!

Dad remained quiet. His silence hurt almost as much as Howard's words. Then both men walked away.

Howard stopped, turned to look at me, and then said, "You need to get out of television. I'm just telling it like it is."

A mid-1970s poll found that Cosell was the most hated sports-caster in America. The same poll said he was the most popular one. Sports fans loved Howard and they hated him. In that moment I was firmly in the "hate" group.

Howard was well known for chastising players and fans who turned to announcing. I figured that Dad would stand up to Howard's attack on my story, that Howard was trying to get a reaction out of him. Neither one of us got what we wanted from Gabe Paul that day. Cosell knocked the wind out of me and I waited for Dad to save me from his vicious tongue. I looked to my dad to be my safety net, but that day he was nowhere to be found.

Not only had Howard knocked me down, but he also said his daughter was better than I was. I knew that it was not true. I do not know what Dad thought, but for the first time I saw how different my dad and Howard were from each other. One man stood up for his daughter when she was absent. The other chose not to stand up for his daughter when she was there. God, I needed to know my dad loved me then.

Howard's quick tongue could strike any man down with a set-up followed by a guaranteed sound bite. Cosell could get angry quickly and turn on someone in an instant whether in print or person-to-person. Talking about himself in an oft quoted interview, Cosell said, "I have been called obnoxious, bombastic, sarcastic, confrontational, and a know-it-all. Of course, I am all of these things." He was interesting. He was contemptible. Yet, he had the viewership and listenership as he interviewed and skewered the popular and the unpopular in his sports broadcasts. He once said, "I don't regard myself as a rabid fan at all. I couldn't care less who wins what game. To me it's the people, the way men react under pressure, the quality of courage."

My dad knew this about his friend. Somehow, he was able to focus on the "whole donut" of this relationship in much the same way as he did in his partnership with George Steinbrenner. He got something out of standing down to these men that he did not get when he stood up to them. If Howard wanted something from Gabe he got it, just as did George.

When it came to his daughter, Howard behaved in a way that ran counter to his public personality. Howard encouraged his daughter, and he was very open about the support he gave to her in her career. My dad operated differently when it came to family. He hated the idea of nepotism and worked to avoid any appearance of favoritism. My dad had the intelligence and mental preparation of a championship ballplayer and the emotional availability of a closed book. I was not able to tell him then how I felt or what I needed. I am doing it now.

Dear Dad,

The boys always said that all you ever did was love me, Dad. I didn't know it. It would have been better if you came back after Howard left and we could have talked. There would have been no doubt then. You knew what his evil words could do to a person's spirit. You were there when he berated Don Meredith and Frank Gifford, and you saw their performance turn inward. Was that what you wanted me to do, lose some of my spirit and personal style? Didn't I deserve your words?

You always said actions speak louder than words. In this case, your silence was deafening and demoralizing. Howard's cruelty went unchecked by the one man who should have been my hero.

For years I wondered why you didn't come back for me. I needed you so much. All I wanted was some affirmation from you about following my dreams, even if others did not think I was "good enough." No matter if I was up or down, I wanted to know that I could count on you.

I needed to know that you loved me. I still do.

I love you Dad,

Jennie

7
The Mouth That Roared

Billy Martin specialized in the unexpected. It might have been a simple change in the batting order, an unexpected bunt, or an offhand remark. Knowing Billy as I do, I am certain that he appreciated Dad as a go-between, and at the same time he played it to his advantage; he respected Dad for his baseball knowledge, and he played him against George. Like Dad, he would make changes to his game that few believed in until they saw them work for the win.

The team rebounded in so many ways throughout these and other conflicts. Despite nearly losing his job on many occasions, Billy was not fazed. In a series of choices that followed the New York Yankees run up to the championship, I watched Billy Martin defy my dad's power. When it came to the dynamics between Billy and George, or later Billy and Reggie Jackson, Dad was there for both men. He would let them scrap about it. Then, Dad, serious and kind, would move in to help resolve the issue in a way that was best for the team. Later, when pressed by the media, Dad downplayed many of these struggles and conflicts when he said, "The internal conflicts were not that different from the quarrels and fights that arise within a family. I think there is a greater respect around for one another," he said. "When you go through things, and you come through them, I think it helps the situation. Everybody here has gone through a lot."

By then the same was true for our father-daughter relationship. Dad and I had gone through a lot as individuals touched by the Yankees, becoming out of touch with one another and our respective needs in our changing relationship. I saw Martin demand respect and not get it. I saw Dad cross the line to show that he was the dominant one controlling their relationship. I saw — felt really — Billy turn it into disrespect of me. As the season wore on and George turned up the pressure, Billy drank more and more. Billy gave me many reasons to leave — all those women, his volatility, the alcoholic outbursts when he did not have the space to process the emotions of the game or demands of running the Yankees the way Gabe Paul and George Steinbrenner wanted.

As a sports reporter who was also Gabe's daughter, I saw these battles from a unique perspective. I was knowledgeable in many sports, having paid my dues covering the local and high school levels and major features for Metromedia, Warner Brothers, HBO, CBS, and NBC. Gabe and Billy knew the game of baseball like no others, and yet somehow when it came to relationships both men missed the ball with me. They would push me and themselves to the limit, and when I was at my breaking point, they'd pull back. It didn't matter if you were a player, a girl friend, or a daughter.

When we were together, Billy and I never discussed Yankee strategy. Many times we talked about Mickey. Billy was protective of Mickey, like a big brother, and yet he wanted to be patted on the back for helping Mantle. Billy would say, "Mickey can't handle his money. I mean he is always giving out $100 tips to the flight attendants on planes, and I have to get him to stop that. I tell him all the time he just can't do that or he will wind up with nothing." It was somehow endearing that Billy thought that he was qualified to look out for his friend's finances.

Then there were the nights we talked about feelings. We challenged one another as we were kindred spirits and fighters. We spoke our own truth, and I felt protected and in a strange sense loved. He drank. We slept together. We had a connection that would linger, and his beady little eyes would draw me in whether I would see him at the stadium or the next week after a game. Our relationship was magically freeing. I was Dad's Yankee Princess, but Billy was no prince and this was not a fairy tale romance. I liked that he was winning, and I always gravitated to the best. He made me feel important and accepted. He did for me exactly what I wanted my dad to do for me. He listened, then he pushed me.

With Billy, I always felt that he had my best interests at heart the way he did for his players. Deep down I believed he wanted me to succeed, to win. With Dad, I wasn't so sure. I wanted to believe that he would have liked me to accomplish something, to be my best. His need for control on how the game played out in my life may have been silent, but it was very much present.

I met Billy's second wife Gretchen by chance one day. She must have been pained by Billy's infidelities over the years, and I didn't want her to know that I was one of Billy's girls. I found I didn't like that thought and began to see the negatives of the affair. I had come to believe that I was no different from other women my age — I created relationships with men based on having an empty heart one minute only to be filled the next with the perfect "one." I fell "in love" for six months until I figured out that there was another woman, or until I heard "I love you but I am not in love with you." I had been doing the same thing on and off for three years with Billy, pretending it didn't matter that we didn't have a true relationship. I vowed then to walk away from Billy Martin for good.

My "away game" did not go as well as I hoped. In fact, my determination to stay away from Billy Martin lasted about as long as most healthy diets. I ended up in Billy Martin's bedroom again and again.

It was such a familiar place for me to be that, frankly, it became more comfortable to be with the wrong person in the wrong situation than to do something about it. It was easier to stick with

Billy, the well-known devil. If I pressed Dad for advice he would throw out one of his "Paulisms" that I knew by rote. I could count on that. To me, the words were as shallow and unfeeling as the relationships and choices that I repeatedly made.

I wish I could have spoken to my father more when he was alive so that we might have worked things out better. It is a regret that will haunt me always.

Looking to the future, Dad, George and Billy all wanted free agent Don Gullett since he beat them in the World Series. With free agency a reality, a dozen marquee players became available, including shortstop Bobby Grich, outfielder Joe Rudi, and outfielder Reggie Jackson, all of the Oakland A's. Billy wanted Bobby Grich and Joe Rudi, and Dad agreed. There were holes in the roster, and each man — George, Dad, and Billy — wanted to be the one to claim that they had made the Yankees champions.

That's when George weighed in. "I want Reggie Jackson. He is a star. We need a star, who can bat clean-up," George said to Dad and Billy. Dad didn't say much according to his diary, though he wanted to sign Bobby Grich as a free agent to play shortstop. Steinbrenner wanted Reggie Jackson because, he said, "his dynamic nature would attract fans." Dad's files showed that he and George both decided Reggie could add value to the team.

In November, soon after the 1976 World Series defeat to the Reds, Dad signed both Don Gullett and free agent Reggie Jackson for $2.96 million. Reggie would be there for spring training. Bucky Dent, whom Dad acquired in a trade with the White Sox, would be on the roster the following season as well. The future was full of promise. But Billy Martin and George Steinbrenner felt that the Yankees needed a better shortstop, and they were willing to trade rookie pitcher Ron Guidry to get him. My dad put his foot down.

"Over my dead body," he said. "Ron Guidry is as good as anybody in the league." Dad somehow knew that Guidry had not reached his full potential yet. He fought hard and convinced Steinbrenner and Martin. In April of 1977, the Yankees got Bucky Dent and they kept Guidry. The White Sox got Hoyt, Gamble, Polinsky, and $250,000 cash. In one of several trades that would validate what Dad could do, Guidry's performance in the 1977 World Series would prove essential to the victory-seeking Yankees management.

Publicly Dad commented, "The thing we've got here is a willingness to gamble. First of all, you have to have the wherewithal. The club's got money and George is a gambler. You've got a situation where you have an eraser on your pencil. You can afford to make mistakes. You don't want to make them, but one or two mistakes aren't going to put you out of business." Privately though, in his taped journal, his frustration boiled over: "This guy takes full credit for all the trades, but never says he was under suspension when we got Randolph, Ellis and Brett or that he wanted Guidry out of there in Fort Lauderdale when he said Guidry didn't have any guts, and then wouldn't take the responsibility for wanting to trade him."

Meanwhile, Martin and Steinbrenner continued to make the headlines with their volatile flare-ups, while Dad quietly umpired the disagreements behind the scenes, saving Billy's job yet again. Dad became the arbitrator, striving to keep the team focused, making effective personnel decisions, and handling the myriad responsibilities like concessions and ticket sales, which George had managed to place on his shoulders. The New York Yankees were Dad's team on paper and in the front office, but the diplomatic abilities of Henry Kissinger would have been challenged by the reality of Dad's daily life. Dad's private files include conversations like this:

"Talk to him," George would order. "Tell him what I want." The "him," of course, was Billy.

Dad would dutifully talk to Billy that night or the next game. His advice was: "You manage like Billy Martin manages. Don't try to be anybody else."

Sooner or later, George would explode. "Did you talk to him?"

"I talked to him," Dad would say.

To a reporter, Billy said, "I could always talk to Gabe, but sometimes it's hard for me to talk to George because we are both the same stubborn."

As the season wore on, the conflicts between George and Billy escalated. Dad meanwhile felt the pressure of the job and the headlines. Still he, Billy and George had one thing in common: They wanted to win more than anything else. When George became frustrated after any loss, he would look to place blame.

What surprised me the most about Dad was that he also had difficulty in his relationship with Billy Martin. The way that Billy conducted himself in and out of the locker room disappointed Dad in so many ways. He liked what Billy knew and what he did, but questioned his character. Despite these feelings, Dad encouraged Billy to be who he was, and made sure Billy knew he would not abandon him.

My dad's diary had this comment on Billy Martin:

He has guts. Maybe that's it. I've been trying to put my finger on it, detect the indefinable something that makes him a winner that stimulates ballplayers. I can't pinpoint it. Managing is other things than tactics. I know that is the thing most commonly criticized, but it is the least important. Most tactics are elementary and managers will do the same things, the same plays, except when they are frustrated and lose confidence. That is when a manager is pressing. He is afraid for his job. Billy Martin doesn't succumb to that kind of pressure. You must have the guts to do what you want to do and not worry about what anybody will think of your judgment. Nobody can say Billy hasn't got guts.

Dad saw Billy as an exceptional skipper. In the files he saved with his diary, Dad wrote, "Billy has the ability to stimulate. He can bring together a club in turmoil. It rubs off even on those who despise him. He has been compared to Durocher, but that's not accurate. Durocher was much easier to analyze. You could figure what made him tick. Martin is much more difficult. What can I say? He passes the test of close inspection. He's fearless and doesn't worry about consequences."

Through it all, Dad's respect and affection for Billy Martin grew in a way that I doubt he anticipated. Dad took care of Billy Martin and protected him, but sometimes Billy didn't return the respect and Dad would fight him on it. Dad's files reveal that on one occasion, for example, Billy accused Dad of not cooperating with him. The two strong-willed men fought constantly for control of the roster, but this time Billy charged that because my dad was refusing to add a 25th player to the roster the team was suffering. According to Dad's diary, he wanted to call up Dell Alston while Billy wanted Elrod Hendricks.

Gabe was furious that Billy wasn't being a team player. Gabe the trader, the consummate public relations man and baseball professional, knew how to respond. Dad invited Billy to make a case for his choice. When Billy chose not to show up for their meeting, Gabe tried to contact him. Billy feigned a lack of availability at first and then confusion over the scheduled meeting. Without consulting Billy, Gabe called up Dell Alston from Syracuse after confirming his plan with George. Dad then sent a note to Billy and released a statement to the press.

BILLY MARTIN

GABE PAUL   May 11, 1977

I was quite surprised and disappointed yesterday when you didn't show up for the 12:00 o'clock appointment you and I had. You recall I called you from Tampa and left a message for you to call me after the Sunday game, May 8th, which you did and we set up a tentative appointment for Monday afternoon , May 9th at the Stadium. I told you there were some things I wanted to discuss with you and that these things should not be discussed on the telephone and I was very anxious to see you. We set up a tentative appointment in the afternoon and you were to call me and tell me what time you would be here at the Stadium. You also said that you would be at the Hotel until the time you come here because you had to pack, etc. I tried several times to get you and finally did get you made in the afternoon and told you how important it was that we get together. You said that when the game against the Mets was cancelled, that you made other arrangements and could not possibly get there that day but would definitely be at the Stadium 12:00 o'clock(Tues) I impressed upon you how important I felt it was and I would be willing to go over to Jersey and meet you half way. You said"please don't do that, I will definitely meet you tomorrow without fail at 12:00 o'clock and we can spend a couple of hours together." So that's the way we left it.

Tomorrow (Tuesday) came and I waited and I waited. I would not go to lunch even though I am required to eat regularly because of the recovery period I am in. I never did talk to you until I called you in Seattle at 10:30 our time. In that conversation, it seemed that we had never had a previous conversation, because you wanted to know what there was that we could not cover on the telephone and you asked why I did not come out to Seattle.

Billy, we have got to work together and baseball must be No. 1. When we have something to discuss, we should discuss it. I don't think breaking all appointments is any way to insure the proper communications between us.

You said you wanted an extra player. I was trying to work out something for the extra player and I feel if you did come to the office either Monday or Tuesday, that the extra player would have been added to the roster. You have complained in the past that you were not "in" on some things. How can you be "in" when you don't keep appointments?

Memo from Gabe Paul to Billy Martin

May 13, 1977

STATEMENT BY GABE PAUL, PRESIDENT

The Yankees have recalled Dell Alston from Syracuse to bring the active roster to the maximum limit of 25. Alston is batting a torrid .338 at Syracuse and the speedster has stolen 11 bases in 19 games. Both of those totals lead the club.

The decision on the 25th player was delayed pending disposition of various negotiations with other clubs and examination of the players at Syracuse. Certain comments directed at Mr. George Steinbrenner, the Club's Principal Owner, by Manager Billy Martin concerning his alleged failure to add a 25th player are totally inaccurate and unfounded.

The facts of the matter are that the addition of the 25th player has been under consideration for several days. The manager, Billy Martin, was asked to report to my office on May 10th, prior to the club leaving for Seattle and at such time the determination of the 25th player was to be made. He agreed to be there. However, Billy failed to show up for the meeting with me. If we had had that conference as scheduled, the 25th player would have been added and the matter would have been settled then and there.

The examination of the performances at Syracuse revealed that Elrod Hendricks is currently batting .105 and it is my feeling that if we need a left-handed pinch hitter we should add one who has been performing more capably at this time. That is why the decision on Alston.

Frankly, if we have to depend on a player hitting .105 at Syracuse to enable us to beat an expansion club, we are indeed in bad trouble. I feel Hendricks will recover from this depressive period, but unless and until he does, we cannot expect him to fill our needs.

The reason for the two losses in Seattle was strictly a matter of too many errors in the field (6) and inconsistent pitching.

Statement by Gabe Paul

Billy did get Elrod, but as Dad had predicted, Hendricks was not a good choice for the Yankees, and he was sent back down to Triple A in Syracuse after the Series. Dad disagreed with Billy on many things, but he had to admit that Hendricks was right on one point. Elrod was an admirer of Billy Martin and called him an expert at "roster management, player positioning and all forms of game strategy" in the same league as rival manager Earl Weaver. I think that admiration for Billy's skills helped Dad and Billy still get along with each other many years later.

All this happened at a time when Dad had to constantly rein in George Steinbrenner. George liked to think of himself as the only boss. So did Billy. Gabe believed neither man could do what he wanted and be a winner without him.

Who knows if the sporting world would have watched as closely as it did if George, Billy, and Dad were running the Indians or the Tigers? But since it was the Yankees, the drama found its way into the papers every day. George gave everyone indigestion. Each of the three, including my dad, thought he was the most important part of the Yankees' success. Billy and George had massive egos. Dad had baseball smarts and great people skills and an ego. This trio came together in a crucible in which each man simmered just below the boiling point, but the combination of the three created gold for the team as a whole.

Dear Dad,

I remember one day at Yankee Stadium when walking to your office through the press gate a guy said to me, "Hey, I am Liza Minelli's agent. She wants tickets." I came right up to you and said, "Dad, Liza Minelli's agent is downstairs and he wants tickets".

You laughed and said, "Jennie, if Liza wanted tickets, I would have received a phone call." It did not take me long to see that that was the way New York was.

I was a woman in her 20's living there and left to deal with the toughness alone to learn my own lessons. Some of those lessons I did learn, but not without some scars and residual effects that even today make me feel left out. I still get people who think I was spoiled or am not telling the truth when I mention who I knew or who was in my circle of friends. That makes it hard to fit in because I feel different. The one thing you did say to me was, "You can count your friends on one hand." You were so right. That is why I turned to Billy repeatedly.

I know for many women making a life around a man is their dream. I did not want to give up control of my life that easily. And yet, that is exactly what I did when I found myself with the wrong man. Dad, I needed you to tell me how to form, keep, and end relationships with men until the right one came along for me. I could not do it with Billy. As much as he loved me, I know he used me, too.

I wish you had paid attention to how much I wanted you to just talk to me, instead of dismissing me with noncommittal responses or one of your "Paulisms."

You were the one I counted on to understand my life — the one who was my safety net. Others put me in celebrity status and were often jealous of what they thought I had. That jealousy many times turned into a mean-spirited anger for something I did not understand, so you were the one person I thought I could count on to help me with this. You were too busy with trades and fighting your battles. I might not have not turned to unhealthy men if we had had the bond I was seeking but did not know how to ask for.

George knew how to ask you for help with Billy, and Billy worked it. You believed that you could keep George and Billy in check, when in truth the reverse was true. I saw the way you tried to control Billy and at the same time give him room to maneuver. I wanted you to give me room and do the same for me. People took advantage of me, and I was vulnerable.

Years later, I have learned that being controlling does not work. People make you pay when you force them to do something that they do not want to do. Was I trying to make you pay for trying to control me by doing the opposite of what I knew you would want for me? When it came to relationships some would say I am a shrink's dream. Maybe I am, or maybe I am just a daughter who needed her Dad.

I love you,

Jennie

8
Clash of the Titans' Egos

Spring training in 1977 brought a public battle between George Steinbrenner and Billy Martin in the New York Yankees' clubhouse near St. Petersburg, Florida. Steinbrenner left in a huff, spouting that the team was not ready, mentally or physically. Dad talked him out of firing Billy that day as he had on several other occasions, and would do again. But George couldn't leave without having the upper hand. First, he tried to put Martin in his place when he told the man point blank, "You're coasting on last year's pennant. Forget it. The first year you win, it's easy. It's ten times tougher to repeat. I want to keep you here, but don't let me down this time. You push me to the wall again, and I promise you, I'll throw you over it."

Later, through Dad and Billy's assistant coaches, George raised the stakes. He questioned the decisions of his team manager and pushed for a batting order that positioned Reggie Jackson, his big dollar free agent, for more RBIs. Billy was batting Reggie fifth behind Chris Chambliss. George wanted Reggie batting fourth. Billy knew that Reggie had the potential to bring more power to the Yankees' hitting, and just didn't like it when George tried to dictate his line-up. Game strategy and team discipline, that was his job. To Billy, George did not know anything about baseball, which made it worse. Martin objected to this pressure from George in the same way that he resented Steinbrenner's parading through the locker room. Billy and Dad understood the unwritten rules of winning and losing; George seemed not to care.

Billy Martin was jealous of the attention Reggie got, as were some of the other players. George seemed to enjoy the conflict, but he reached out to players and the team captain Thurmon Munson to get their buy-in on his decision about Jackson. Chris Chambliss, who had the cleanup spot, was not happy about Jackson, but since Munson did not see Jackson as a threat he backed off.

Meanwhile, George also fed the press stories that sometimes skewed reality in his favor. Every now and then Dad would set them straight the way he did when he said, "It's wrong to say that signing Reggie was George's decision. We decided whom to bring on together. We talked it over, like scouts with a ballplayer, and we made a decision. I made the first contact with Reggie. George worked out the deal. Now it is just a matter of making the right fit with the talent and management."

I knew Billy pretty well by this time, as did Dad. Billy was in the first year of a three-year contract renewal that he had just signed with Dad. The pennant win the previous year united them in their respect for one another's strengths and a healthy fear of their weaknesses. Dad knew that Billy did not respond well to threats to his position or attempts to control him. Billy didn't believe that Reggie Jackson had earned the special attention and treatment he received from George. He did not want Reggie to play more than other team members did, especially the ones who were hustling.

Billy liked hustle. Thurman Munson, for example, played hurt and he worked out every day. The fact that Munson had issues with George over the money that Reggie was making earned him some favor from his manager. It was obvious to Dad that it was true Reggie had not met Billy's expectations, but the real fight was about attention from George.

When the media portrayed Reggie as more important than Billy and the rest of the team, it stuck in Billy's craw. The Yankees had won the '76 pennant without Reggie. Munson, who had batted .300, was the team leader. At the same time, George and Dad also realized that a rivalry between Reggie and Thurman would sell tickets. Baseball was a business after all, and selling tickets was the objective. Both Dad and George pushed Billy to play Reggie in the field more. Billy was a pitching and defense manager while Reggie was an average fielder at best. Billy played the men whom he felt would help him win. He often would insert Reggie as the team's designated hitter, which Reggie felt was a slap in the face.

Billy wanted to motivate Reggie, but the Yankees' newest free agent was not responding the way most other players had; Reggie saw Martin's approach as disrespectful. For a time, Reggie kept his feelings to himself, but the tension hung over the team. Billy interpreted Reggie's attitude as a lack of willingness to work on his game.

Reggie and Billy were at loggerheads before that memorable series of games began in Boston in June of 1977. The fact that Reggie played the race card or flashed a wad of bills whenever he believed that he was wrongly singled out, or treated as less significant than he thought he was in the Yankee organization, made it easier for Billy to point his finger at the player rather than any conflict in himself. It was a pressure cooker inside the organization. Martin stood up for each Yankee, except for Reggie Jackson. The Yankees had become a group of individuals that looked like a team only because they dressed alike. Take away the uniforms and they were an unruly mob of egos.

That weekend in Boston, the tension between the rival Boston Red Sox and New York Yankees was thick, but it was nothing compared to the hostility between Reggie and Billy. The pressure showed and the Yankees played poorly in Friday's game as the Red Sox won 9-4. The fans expected to see more from pennant winners and World Series contenders. The disgusted Yankee fans threw trash on the field and shouted at both teams words that did not sound much like "baseball, apple pie, and Chevrolet."

Dad and I missed the game Friday night in Boston. The TWA flight that I was working was not scheduled to land until much later. Dad was still in New York, but we would both be there the next day when the spectacle happened at Fenway Park.

I was enjoying my dual career, and the human-interest sports stories I was bringing in thanks to my flying job with TWA continued to pay off as I found myself in the places where the stories were before they happened. Sometimes the story was closer to home than I expected. Friday, June 17, 1977, was one of those days. When I walked into my apartment after a long flight, Reggie Jackson was in my kitchen kissing my roommate. Reggie could have gone anywhere after the Yankees lost the first game in the three-game series with the Red Sox. It was a gamble when he chose to come to my apartment. I was the daughter of the man who had brought him to the Yankees. More than that, I was Yankee manager Billy Martin's on-and-off girlfriend.

At the time, I believed that my dad was the only one in the New York Yankee organization that did not seem to know Billy and I had been together. Reggie knew. To this day, I do not know if Reggie came there to see me and was surprised at my absence or if he was innocently visiting my roommate. It did not look that innocent when I walked into my place in Boston. The stove was not on, but it was hot in there!

"Ahh shit! You have got to leave!" I said angrily. I started scolding him. "Why do you only go out with white girls? Isn't that reverse discrimination?"

It was not Reggie's night at Fenway, and things were going about the same in my apartment. He would not score there either.

He had not yet earned the nicknames of Mr. October or Mr. June. If anything, he looked like Mr. Embarrassed, as my roommate flitted away, giggling. "If Dad knew…ugh this is too weird. Why are you even here? You know, Billy might show up."

Off the field, Reggie made his situation with the Yankees more difficult than it had to be by the things he said and did. In my view, being with a white girl in 1977 was another way Reggie would bring trouble to himself and to the team. The Yankees did not need any more distractions. I wanted to get him out of my apartment. Reggie's being there put me in a very compromising position, too.

I said, "C'mon, I'll take you home."

On the ride back to his hotel, Reggie started to tell me about the game and the fans throwing junk and booing. His teammates avoided him in the locker room after the game, just like they had in the games before and in New York. I felt sorry for him. I knew what it was like to feel unloved by the people you thought were your friends or fans. I said, "Reggie, you are taking it way too personally. Yankee fans are quick to react. They get emotional at Red Sox games. It's the Curse of the Bambino," I offered in an attempt at levity.

He sat there, brooding.

I kept after him, trying to gloss over that the way he played that night only made things worse. Finally, I said, "Yankee and Red Sox fans sure have a unique definition of sportsmanship." I laughed.

He didn't laugh. Reggie just nodded. Suddenly something clicked inside of me and my reporter instincts kicked in. I knew Reggie had been avoiding the press. If you were on talk radio in Boston, you knew about the challenges that your peers and rivals faced.

"You owe me an interview for being here," I said. "I'll be at Fenway Park tomorrow at 9 a.m. with a film crew. Make sure you're there."

He got out of the car.

"Are you going to be there?" I asked.

No answer.

The next day I showed up during batting practice with a film crew from the local network affiliate. Reggie was there, and I imagine we drew a bit of attention to ourselves. I interviewed him in the Red Sox dugout, starting with some very basic questions about the Friday night game. It was boring. No human interest. Not my usual style.

Reggie Jackson and Jennie Paul

I thought I might end up with a soft feature for "Sunday Sports Extra." Maybe I could work some of the points into my radio sports trivia show later that week, like how many times he had turned down interview requests. I thought his answers were stupid.

Then Reggie said something that I thought was even more simple-minded. With the cameras rolling, Reggie looked at me and said, "I don't want to be a Yankee anymore."

"What?!" I said. "Why not?"

He followed with angry remarks about being tired of not getting the recognition and respect that he deserved. The Yankees owed him. He was entitled. I forgot about the cameras for a minute. I slipped into daughter of the team president and general manager mode. Hands on my hips, I said, "Well Reggie, what do you expect? You come in after the team is already righting itself from a slump that started when we were all kids. They were making history before Dad signed you, and in the first few days that you are here, you imply that they cannot win without you. That is pretty bad, Reggie, but showing off how much money you make while holding back at bat — I don't think that is in your contract. Oh, yeah, you told me about that last night, remember? You don't even look like you are working at it or for it."

Okay, it was not the best way to get a story, but I felt the need to say something after his snotty remark. Reggie shut down. Not surprisingly, I didn't get much for my feature or trivia show after that. I didn't think much of the interview, and it would not have been special if Reggie had his head in the game instead of the other place that comes to mind. When the interview ended, I took the film out of the camera and couriered it to New York for Sunday's show.

Within a few hours, I was back at the stadium looking for my dad. He was sitting near the dugout. No longer in sports broadcaster mode, I was simply a girl on a social outing with her Dad.

I was there for the same reason all the other fans came. They had been arriving in droves. We all wanted to see these archrivals duke it out on the field, not in bench-clearing brawls, but rather like a baseball game ought to be played. I wanted to see home runs and great plays. I wanted a close game where the victor emerged at the last moment. The city was abuzz in part because of what happened the night before, but also because of the long-standing rivalry.

Jackson, who usually took his emotions out on the ball, instead held back at the bat, and it was obvious. Then when he was in the outfield, he let a ball get by him that Billy was sure a more focused right fielder would have stopped. Billy Martin pulled Reggie Jackson off the field in mid-inning. Billy was furious that Reggie failed to hustle on a ball hit to the outfield, sending in Paul Blair as a replacement. Reggie was flabbergasted and disgusted, and he showed it by his slow exit from the field. Clearly embarrassed, Reggie said something to Billy as he walked toward his place on the bench. The remark was the final straw and the manager went to take a swing at Reggie. This time, it was Billy's swing that missed. Reggie poked fun at Billy's loss of control and, had it not been for Yogi Berra or Elston Howard, there might have been an all-out brawl.

Jackson did not take humiliation from anyone, especially Martin. While accounts differ on exactly what was said to whom before, during, and after Billy's decision, the cameras caught all the action. Jackson was hustled off the field and into the clubhouse. He left through a side door while the Yankees were still on the field.

The epic skirmish happened in a place and between two teams where the level of competitiveness was unlike any other in major league baseball history. The Yankee-Red Sox rivalry was bitter and long lasting, traceable to the day Harry Frazee traded Babe Ruth to the Yankees some 50 years before. Back then, the Red Sox fans did not object. They believed that Ruth was no longer giving the Red Sox his best effort. The trade proved to be a bad bet for the Red Sox as Ruth answered this home team's rejection with the "Curse of the Bambino," bringing home five World Series titles with the Yankees. Reggie was not Ruth, but he would fire up the Bronx in the post season, and the Yankees would do much to enforce the Curse. The Red Sox would not see another championship until 2004.

All eyes were on Dad. The media wanted to hear what the Yankees had to say about Reggie. They wanted to know what would happen to Billy. Dad promised to give them the details after he and George had discussed it more. The reporters respected Gabe for his focus on the team since he had made it clear that he would deliver a story as he had on many other occasions. The Yankees best interests would be served as would the sportswriters, Dad proclaimed privately to the Boss and the beat respectively.

Unknown to most at that time, TV 5 already had a story, one that would prove to be a spark to the dynamite fuse of my relationship with Dad. For now, though, the damage was still sitting in an unedited can.

Reggie had not spoken to the press since May 1977 after Robert Ward, a reporter from *Sport* magazine wrote an article based on conversations with Reggie during the Yankees spring training in Ft. Lauderdale. Instead of taking responsibility for his comments in the magazine, Reggie accused the writer of misquoting him, and then he told the other reporters he wouldn't talk to them. According to Reggie, he told Ward that the Yankees had lost the Championship to the Reds in the previous year because they were missing one thing. He pointed to his drink and alleged that Ward inferred the rest in this quote: "This team, it all flows from me. I'm the straw that stirs the drink. Maybe I should say me and Munson, but he can only stir it bad."

Reggie's teammates were furious. Reggie denied saying it that way, but the quote took on a life of its own. Munson, a team leader, had been a supporter of Reggie at the beginning. Billy Martin, of course, was not, and the tension continued to escalate after the June dugout fight. The consensus among reporters on the beat was that Dad and George did little to reduce the conflicts within the team. I was there, and I know that Dad did a lot; Reggie knew it, too.

I don't think Billy thought about the TV cameras that day. In those days there was no delay like there is today. Producers did not have a chance to cut to a different camera before the public saw. We all saw it like it was, and we saw it when it happened. Steinbrenner, who was in Cleveland that day, saw it at the same time as the reporters. They were rushing to the pay phones to be the first to call in the story. Some from the press corps clamored toward Dad instead of Ma Bell. Phil Pepe caught Dad as he was quickly making his way to the owner's suite. I heard Dad say, "I'll talk with both Martin and Jackson later in a calmer atmosphere in an effort to resolve the problem." Dad hustled to the owner's suite. He wanted to be the first to tell George, but the operator put George through as Dad walked through the door, and I followed.

"Our team is out of control! Gabe, fire Billy now!" Click. George was gone.

Dad knew it was only for a minute. He was standing there with the receiver in his hand. George would call back. That much was certain. Meanwhile, Reggie had left the dugout and the stadium. Billy had retreated to the locker room. Just then, the phone rang. It was not George.

It was TV 5. Unlike the rest of the press, they did not want to talk to Dad. The Sports Extra producer wanted to talk to me. My producer was excited. "Jennie, this is huge," he said. "Reggie hasn't talked to the press in weeks. I don't know how you got the interview with Reggie Jackson! It is great. We are running it Sunday on

"Sports Extra." You are in Boston, now right? Is your Dad there? We are trying to get George. If you can get any more, get it here by midnight. I'll get it in!" The producer was gone.

Caught somewhere between being the Yankee Princess when all hell broke loose and the big time sports broadcaster I wanted to be, I froze under Dad's burning glare. When I sent the tape to New York earlier, I thought it was a disappointing piece. I did not know what I had at that time. I made an offhand remark, but the fight had cast a new light on the series of sound bites and pictures cycling through the editing machine in the studio in New York.

Dad heard me talking. He was about to say something when the phone rang again. This time it was George. With a fixed stare, Dad pulled the phone away from his ear. It was not for my benefit. George was very loud. "Is that any way for a balanced manager to appear on national television!" he yelled.

Dad spoke to George, trying to calm him down. There was no emotion in Dad's voice, which was not completely out of character for him. Dad said he would talk to Reggie and Billy at breakfast, and George before and after that.

Click. George was off the line again, satisfied for the time being.

I did not know if Dad knew about my interview with Reggie. He often seemed to have his ear to the ground. For a minute, I just stood there. I thought about getting Dad's comments to add to George's remarks. It would be a good way to punch up my interview, not that it needed any more emotion. I wanted to talk to Dad — he would rebalance my world and, in fact, the story, I thought.

Dad had barely replaced the phone after George hung up when it rang again. It was George again. The station had reached him. I heard him say that I had taped an interview with Reggie and the station planned to air it in an unfavorable light. Now Dad knew for sure what I had done before the game. He did not have his poker face on. I was excited and fearful all at once as he put the phone on the hook. Before I could say anything, Dad demanded that I get the film back and not air it.

"What! No, not again, Dad. Do you realize that this story is as big as Catfish Hunter was to you? My producer said this is my big break. Reporters wait their whole careers for a story like this. It is my ticket to a network position. I want it." I was determined to win this game.

"Dad, I got this interview on my own. I followed my instincts, like you always said. Nobody used me to get to you, Dad!" I shrilled.

Dad knew I wanted to win his approval and love more than anything. At that moment he played his cards brilliantly. Softly, calmly, and in a very strained voice Dad said, "Jennie, I know what Reggie said. I don't know why he said it to you. You know he has not been talking to the press. He probably didn't know that the cameras were on. He was talking to you like a friend. You know how it is when a friend talks to you. They say things that they don't expect you to print or broadcast to others outside your confidence."

I forgot about Reggie for a minute, and remembered what Sheila Moran had done to me when she cared more about the story than our relationship. It had only been a few years but the pain was still there. Instantly crushed by what Dad said, I felt my dream slipping out of my fingers. The fact that Dad actually understood what had happened then went over my head. I didn't think about it until years later.

Suddenly, I went from feeling elated about how close I was to reaching my dream, to feeling like a little girl who had done something very wrong to her parents. I didn't feel like a reporter who had a great story, even though it was certainly true. The phone rang again. It was my producer. I took the call. I barely got out a hello when he said rather tensely, "Jennie, did you get anything from your Dad?" Everyone was under pressure. It was evident in his tone and my reaction.

"Ah Yeaaah…." I snapped out of it enough to be present for the phone conversation, while Dad stayed there for a minute, clearly impatient with the interruption.

"Good, because Reggie is talking to one of our guys now. Not just our people. Everyone. No one has what we have! We've got a TV 5 ratings victory here, little girl."

Men said that to women sports reporters in 1977. It was tough to be a woman in this business then. Any other time, I might have objected to the remark and stood up for myself, but at that moment I didn't feel like I could defend anyone, especially not me.

The line went dead.

Dad and I took our attention away from one another and turned up the volume on the television in time to hear Reggie say, "I played ball exactly the way I wanted to."

Dad's face turned red. He looked at me, pleadingly. "You can't air your interview. It will make the Yankees look bad. It will hurt me." His voice trailed off as he left the suite abruptly. The television seemed louder when the door closed behind him. At that time in my career and my relationship with my dad, I feared success almost as much as failure. To say I was now embroiled in conflict as heated and as tense as Reggie and Billy would be a close second to the understatement of the year. I folded. I called my producer. "Don't run the story," I said.

"What, why? If you can't get whatever you are working on in time for the show, we can run a follow-up. This story is not going away quickly. What do you have, anyway?"

"Nothing. You know my dad. I think it will be better for the station if we kill this one."

"Are you shitting me? Do you want to come back to New York full time? This is huge. We can't kill it. You want to hurt yourself, go ahead. I am not taking the hit on this one." Click.

Reggie and Billy were exactly where their actions had put them — in the hot seat, at breakfast with my dad that Sunday morning in his hotel suite in Boston. The last game of that series had yet to be played and my interview with Reggie had not aired on National television yet. By the end of the meal, these men would lay all their cards on the table, and Dad would win. They found common ground if not peace. According to the letter Dad wrote and kept with his files, the meeting was tense. Reggie was quick to accuse Billy of racial remarks. Dad quelled that outburst fast, appealing to both men to cool down and shake hands in honor of the game if not out of respect for one another. The meeting ended well. They finished the series in Boston.

Dad was famous for his breakfast meetings. The Yankees had another game with Boston that day and Dad wanted to make sure that he and Billy and Reggie talked some things out. I wasn't jealous that I was not included in his efforts to straighten things out. It is just something small that he could have done which would have gone a long way to fill the daddy hole that got a whole lot bigger when he told me to kill the story on Reggie.

As it was, I ate alone that morning, and I was left to wonder about what I needed to do to play better. Not unlike Billy and Reggie, we both needed to work on our game, Dad and I. What I really needed from Dad was to be treated the way he treated these ball players. Not with the offhand "Paulisms" — there were plenty of those. For dads and daughters to work through their issues together, one or the other has to have guts, guts like Billy Martin, or perhaps guts like Yogi, who held Billy back when he went after Reggie in the dugout. I had guts. I waited to have what I knew would be a very difficult conversation with Dad, the only man that I loved and hated at the same time.

We spoke after his breakfast meeting. "Dad, looks like they are running that story," I said matter-of-factly. "We can make this better. I know we can. You can give me the interview that you want to give."

Silence.

I started rambling. "You can say what you said to Phil and the others and more. The Yankees already look bad now. Dad, this is a great opportunity. I won't edit anything. Say what you want to say. Let people believe what they want to believe. This is a great chance for you to tell everyone how much you have done for this team. I do not want you to be hurt, Dad."

"I am not saying anything, Jennie. If you cannot keep the story off the air, get yourself out of it," said Dad.

Refusing to comment on a story rarely kept it out of the news when it was bad. It ran that Sunday night.

And then it happened. My taped interview with Reggie had been reduced to little more than a sound bite, which hit national TV, stunning audiences with cutting words straight from Reggie's own mouth: "I don't want to be a Yankee anymore!" After the fuss I made over my Dad's disapproval, my producer reluctantly took my face and name out of the story, but he kept my voice in it. There were some over-the-head shots that the station had not cut. It was clear to everyone watching that I was the one doing the interview. George was not watching. He was on his way to the game in Detroit. He and Dad had a lot to talk about regarding Billy and Reggie. From his hotel suite, Steinbrenner had said, "I think Jackson hustled as much as he could on that questionable play."

Reggie started remembering history in a way that glorified his reality as he became more and more like George Steinbrenner, his biggest supporter. In truth, George's support of Reggie was more about George playing Billy and somewhat about George wanting to be a player and not just the "Boss." Many years later when the book *Reggie* was published, Dad wrote to Jackson, responding to

Reggie's accusing Dad of racism. Although the letter was just between the two of them, I believe it is long enough ago to share here.

July 16, 1985

Mr. Reggie Jackson
California Angels
Anaheim Stadium
Post Office Box 2000
Anaheim, Calif. 92803

Dear Reggie:

I have intended writing you for some time, since reading your book "Reggie," in which you discussed the incident which occurred on Saturday afternoon, June 18, 1977, at Fenway Park, Boston, when Billy Martin took you out of the game in the middle of an inning and substituted Paul Blair for you.

The near fight between you and Billy in the dugout after the move was seen on National Television.

Your description of the breakfast meeting I called for the next morning at 9 A.M., attended by you, Billy, and myself is totally erroneous. When I read your account, I looked at the picture I have in my office of the two of us taken in the clubhouse after the last game of the '77 Series and reread the inscription in your handwriting which said, "To Gabe - Just want U to know I'll too miss those little talks!"

                            Reggie Jackson
                            10-18-77

I'm proud of the many talks we had, but I'm not proud of your description of the breakfast meeting which was pure fiction.

That was a very serious occasion and not the time for levity and the use of the phrases you said I used then. I have used those sayings often, but I did not use them that day. Neither did Billy say, "Get up, boy, I'm going to kick the shit out of you right here."

```
Mr. Reggie Jackson                              Page Two
July 16, 1985


       He did include the word "Boy" in a sentence which caused
you to jump up and say you weren't going to take that crap
from him or anybody else.  I said I didn't think there was
any racial connotation in Billy's remark, and that you should
sit down, cool down, and shake hands with Billy.

       You agreed to do it, then Billy refused to shake hands,
but after several minutes he did shake hands with you and
we resumed the breakfast and conversation, which ended on a
fairly decent note.  Certainly not the way you described it
in that chapter.

       For your information, the breakfast meeting was called
by me, and not at the suggestion or direction of George
Steinbrenner.  I was sitting next to our dugout when the
incident happened, so was familiar with all the circumstances.

       Reggie, I think you owe me an apology.


                              Cordially,



                              Gabe Paul


GP:ptj
```

Letter from Gabe Paul to Reggie Jackson

Sadly, racism was common in many places during the 70s. Dad and George both agreed that prejudice had no place in the Yankee organization. It took awhile, but Dad found a way to motivate Billy and Reggie to play through their pain and abandon their own personal desires and to submit for the good of the team. They were the New York Yankees. People expected them to be better sports.

The following Monday, the reporters found Dad, George, Billy, and Reggie in Detroit. Billy said, "I only ask one thing of my players. Hustle. If they hustle for me, they can play for me. I told them in spring training. I had a meeting. I told them you play only one way, to win. You play hard and give your 100% best."

The reporters found Reggie before the next game. Reggie was "on" again, acting incredulous about the questions from reporters about how Billy handled the game that day. "Why should I second guess the manager? I don't know anything about managing. I know what I have to do. Go out and play to the best of my ability. If they say go home, I go home. If they say play, I play. I'll take the heat," Reggie said.

One asked, "Mr. Steinbrenner, last Saturday you said you believed that Billy is…wait let me get this right, unbalanced. Does he have a future with the Yankees?"

George, unusually restrained, avoided the spotlight, offering up my dad instead when he said, "My contacts with Martin recently have been few and far between. My principal interest is to see the matter resolved one way or another. I want to sit back and enjoy a baseball game on the field again. The decision on whether or not to keep Martin after all that business in Boston is entirely Gabe Paul's. He's the guy right now. I'll stand behind him either way he goes."

Dad was quick to follow George's remark. "There will not be a change in our organization regardless of what has been said. We don't feel there's a better manager than Billy Martin, and we want the Yankees to have the best," Dad said with a smile.

The press did not want to let it go. Controversy sold papers. "I don't always agree with what Billy says or does, but I respect his right to say it," wrote Dad. I thought, "Gosh, Dad, if you would have spoken to me the way you talked about your manager, we might actually have had a better connection."

"There were some things that had to be straightened out, and they were straightened out," Dad said. "From the first pitch till the last out, there's no better manager in baseball than Billy and he's the one we want," he finished, never missing a beat.

"What about tomorrow?" clamored the reporters.

It took some doing to get to this point with Billy and George both making nice in the press. George released seven qualifications for a team manager, and history would continue to refer to it as "the seven commandments." Popular history had it wrong, because in actuality there were nine points of agreement, and Dad had Billy sign them a full two years earlier when Billy first joined the team. (See page 94.) However, Dad's aim was to appease George's desire for discipline and re-establish his need for a patriarchal hierarchy. Dad always kept the original document with his diary; Billy, of course had a copy. He would need to refer to it, Dad was sure.

Billy did get himself under control. His first remarks were devoid of the emotion of 72 hours before. He was almost robotic when he said, "I plan to talk with my right-fielder before today's game and tell him just what is expected of him. I hope that will clear the air."

I think Billy was afraid that he would lose his job. After all, the Yankees were his identity, and fearing that kind of loss can damage a man. Some of the members on the press were disappointed at Billy's calm manner. While Dad and George rarely showed their true feelings, Billy Martin was something else altogether. Now, though, he was uncharacteristically repentant. At the same time, he clearly wanted to convey that he was, in fact, on top of things. Billy explained himself to fans and players through the press, "Nothing is easy when you are a leader. I'm trying to be careful. I don't want the press hurting this club anymore or hurting management. I'm management too." God, I loved that about Billy. You didn't always like what he said or what he did. He told you what he expected of you, and then you knew. You knew what it took for his approval. Moreover, if you didn't know, he would tell you. Dad was like Billy to everyone, it seemed, except me. I never knew what Dad expected.

Reggie had his say, too. "I'll say this and I won't apologize for it later. If George Steinbrenner were a ballplayer, he'd be like Reggie Jackson."

Meanwhile, George proclaimed, "I'm in charge." He told reporters that he, not Gabe, had made the decision to keep Martin. "I didn't know what was happening," George said, "but I don't understand why Gabe didn't know." George was talking about my interview even though the media thought he was referring to the animosity that led to the fight with Reggie and Billy.

"What I saw in Detroit with the Yankees saddened me," George said, "but what upset me the most is what was happening to my team president Gabe Paul. He is supposed to be Billy Martin's superior and the team's general manager."

Anyone who knew George and Billy or my dad knows that what the newspapers print is often only half the story, and sometimes they get it wrong. What George said in public and what he did in private were frequently different. The confrontation that preceded George's public disrespect of Dad was one story that I never knew until Dad's death. I talked to my brother about what he knew, what mother had told him, and explored Dad's diary in an attempt to understand all the undercurrents and behind-the-scenes action. Years later, I learned about what Dad did for me.

George had verbally attacked me after he heard my voice on "Sunday Sports Extra" in the Reggie piece. He turned his anger at the media on me in the same way that he did when the Tricia Nixon story made the papers a few years earlier.

When Dad chose to keep Billy, George could do little since he had stated so publicly that it was Gabe's call. I believe George must have thought that he had Dad right where he wanted him when he made the fight about me.

The line between the New York Yankees and Gabe Paul's family was well defined. George had not crossed it before. When George stepped over it, attacking my reputation, Dad came out fighting. "Don't you ever talk to or about my daughter that way! My family is off-limits."

"Not a bad idea, Gabe. Yankee Stadium is hereby off-limits to your whole family, and particularly your daughter. I am banning her from the Yankees!" said George.

Dad walked out. He got on a plane for Florida, back to Mom, again.

Jennie Paul and Cynthia Andrialis

When George threatened to ban me from Yankee Stadium, I was indignant that he would attempt to thwart me as a sports reporter. Tired of my dad's lack of support, and not yet knowing he had gone home to Florida, I did not consult him on my next move.

At a party after the all-star game, my friend, Cynthia Andri-alis watched as I walked up to Steinbrenner and said, "George, you cannot ban me from the stadium. I am a respected sports journalist. You cannot treat me differently than any other sports reporter!"

Cynthia's eyes just about popped out of her head. George quickly backed down. I figured that I had Steinbrenner where I wanted him. For all his bravado, he had just seen me get airtime with a story he thought he could keep inside the Yankee locker room. To my surprise he was speechless, which was very unusual for George.

George was finally in his place, I thought, and I had put him there. The truth, which I did not learn until long after, was that George was not so much afraid of me as he was of what I might do next. Certainly he was afraid of not having my dad when he needed him the most. He had a pennant to defend and a championship to chase.

I thought the interview with Reggie was a high point for my career until I spent more time talking with Pearl Davis. She said we were alike, Dad and I, She called me "a real whippersnapper." She said, "Oh Jennie, you had guts, girl. You were out there like that, do you understand me?"

"You would always tell Mr. Steinbrenner what you thought and then you would do what you wanted. You didn't realize a lot of stuff, being so young. Your dad loved you, Jennie. He may not have shown it the way you wanted it, although we all saw it. Your Dad protected you from George as best and as long as he could. When the Reggie story broke, he could not calm Mr. Steinbrenner down about you. He certainly tried. Jennie, you and your Dad were always at war with each other and I never understood that. When you were gone, he would always say how much he loved you."

I might have handled some things differently if I had known what Pearl knew. The upheaval and conflict of 1977 hit all our lives. For all the highs and lows, though, it seemed Dad and I barely changed from the combative relationship we had built over the years. All I can do now is say what I could or should have then.

Dear Dad,

As too often before, your words in the midst of what could have been my greatest sports moment seemed calculated to cause me the most pain. I could not understand how Jennie Paul, sports reporter, became responsible for Reggie's behavior because I was there with a camera and a microphone.

Why did you punish me by withdrawing your love and support from me when I was just doing my job? The things you said to me... I never set out to hurt you.

We were on opposite teams in a way, me working for the media and you working for the team. Still we were family, not enemies. You were my foe and my hero, although I saw only the one. You know something Dad? If you had told me what you did about George's crass remarks, or if you had written me a letter like the one that you did to Reggie, correcting my misconceptions, it would have been different between us when you were alive.

Damn it, Dad! Why didn't you tell me that you stood up to George on my behalf? Do you know how many life experiences I would have handled better if I had known where you drew the line between the Yankees and family?

Daughters go through life and expect their fathers to know how they feel, and I think many fathers expect the same from their daughters. If I had known that you had taken a stand for me and walked away from a winning team to defend my honor, I would have been touched more deeply than you can imagine. But all I knew is that you were not by my side backing me up that day.

It pains me that I did not get to thank you for being my hero.

I love you, Dad.

Jennie.

9

The Dream Fulfilled

It didn't take long for George to figure out that he was in trouble after Dad walked out. Admitting it in public was not quite as easy. George continued to berate my dad to the press. "Gabe was a winner last year because I pushed and shoved and forced him to make decisions," George boasted. But when the lights went out and the cameras were off, George was forced to face the truth: He realized he wasn't capable of doing all of the jobs that he had assigned to Dad. He needed my father. Then, George did everything he could to get Dad to come back.

George apologized after Dad flew back to Florida, promising never to say anything about our family or me again. He convinced Dad to return, offering him a chance to see his team through the season and to make all future decisions on Martin and Jackson, all the while dangling the carrot of a new three-year contract that they would put in writing when the time came.

To Dad, keeping to his contract and his word was as important when he owned and ran the Yankees as it was when he had walked away. Tumultuous times did not call for an abandonment of one's values. He could return to the Yankees, if nothing else, based on a principle by which he lived: Stick to it.

Within days, Dad was back and offering his insight to all the speculating reporters while going about running the business of his ball club. Reporters questioned Dad's expectations for his longevity with the Yankees.

"Do you think you will be replaced by someone younger, more forceful?"

Dad laughed. "Oh hell, no!"

Dad was the only one who knew that George came after him when he left, just as he did all the other times. As a master of PR, Dad revealed only what the reporters needed to know for their story. He continued to take questions and on keeping Billy, Dad just said, "Well, no decision is an individual one. We always work as a team." Dad added, "George and I had an agreement on it, and if he didn't think this was the best course, he wouldn't have done it that way. I don't think anyone can accuse him of being a dummy. He felt this was the best way to handle it. I felt it was the best way to handle it and this was the understanding that we had. I'm sure the decision I reached was in agreement with his decision, but if my decision was different than his, I think he still would have carried through," Dad answered.

George continued to back Reggie in a more open and public fashion while Gabe worked to keep each of the men in a place where they could perform and win. It wasn't easy on Dad as the infighting continued. Dad remarked, "Some of the unhappiest players have played the best ball. We judge players by what they do on the field. If we want all nice boys, we'll go on the church steps and collect them. We have controversial players and we have controversial situations. Once in Toronto, I said they have to cut out the bull and play ball and I think they did. Look at our record. We don't always win or play the way people expect, but no one can deny that these boys can play ball."

Writing now from the perspective of 30 years of wondering if Dad loved me, I see the parallels in his view of players and me. He treated us the same. It did not work for me, but it sure did for Dad and Reggie.

Reggie came out swinging for Dad and Billy in a way similar to "The Babe" 50 years before. Accused of being sluggish and not going after the ball the way Billy thought that he should, Reggie had as much to prove as the "Sultan of Swat" did in his day. In September and October of 1977, Reggie delivered. On September 14, Jackson hit a homer off of Reggie Cleveland for a 2-0 win, propelling the Yankees into a pennant contest with Kansas City. The irony of that contest was not lost on Dad.

The Yankees took the American league pennant in 1977, the same as they had the year before. Gabe Paul made the team that would have back-to-back World Series appearances.

Dad said, "I told our guys, we have a World Series now. We have to bear down and forget about all that junk that's going on, and that's what it is…a lot of junk." For a period as brief as Steinbrenner's humility that fall of 1977, the Yankees got along. They played like a team that wanted a World Series championship ring. The media though was not about to let go of the drama between Billy and Reggie and between Billy and George. As it looked more and more promising for the New York Yankees, Dad answered the continued inquiries from the gentlemen of the sports press.

Dad planned to reduce the turmoil if not avoid it altogether; it was time to focus on the business of winning. Steinbrenner uncharacteristically tried to distance himself from the headlines and Billy. He maintained that Dad would make the decision about Martin's future after the 1977 season. No one believed him. The reporters pressed for more. They wanted answers. Would the team and coaching staff stay intact in the post season?

Dad simply stated that the World Series would not be the determining factor in Martin's fate. Whatever happened, whatever he decided, it would be the result of months of reflection. The frequent meetings, diary entries, and the reports of the many times that Dad was drawn into battle with his player and manager confirm that Dad put a lot of time and effort into his diplomacy. Dad didn't say much, preferring to work behind the scenes, until he could no longer avoid public action.

"I don't know that we have to do anything," Dad said. "The only time you sit down and make a judgment is when you think something is wrong. If you do, you have to act on it. If you don't, you leave it alone."

Meanwhile, Thurman Munson, the 1976 World Series MVP, managed to steal a headline or photo op now and then from the Boss, from Billy, and from Reggie. In public, George and Dad downplayed the noise Munson made about wanting to be traded to the Indians or threatening to quit baseball. Privately, Dad told Thurman that he was too valuable to the Yankees to let go, not even to Dad's hometown team, the Indians. Dad made sure that Thurman knew that the 100 homers he had hit in three straight years meant something to Dad and the Yankees. They were in this battle for the championship together. Then he appealed to Thurman's wallet, telling him that Cleveland could not come up with enough money to make it worth it to him.

In the press, Dad was all business on the matter. Unlike George, he gave it to them straight. "When players want to be traded, you take them seriously," Dad said, "but we are not going to make any deals that we don't feel help the Yankees. We'll be glad to accommodate them if the Yankees are helped. I don't see how the Indians can give the Yankees enough to satisfy Thurman Munson's demand to be traded there. It's a pretty damned tough job to strengthen a ball club by trading Munson," Dad finished. No trade.

In October 1977 the Yankees were in their second World Series in as many years, an accomplishment that had eluded them for over a decade. The fans were turned on. Rivals watched. People who previously had cared little for the sport or these teams couldn't wait to see what would happen next. Living up to his reputation, Billy Martin motivated his team with the come-from-behind tactics that riveted fans and rivals alike. With a highly volatile, newsworthy season behind them, some were watching to see what Billy would do next. Would there be another big fight? It seemed imminent, and few were surprised at a blow-up in the hotel during the series or the extensive media coverage that followed. The ever-present possibility sold papers and guaranteed airtime.

Dad was animated as I had never seen him, thrilled as a World Series championship win became possible after Yankee victories in Games 1 and 3. At the same time, he was careful not to let his optimism overrule his judgment. Reggie hit a home run in Game 4 and they won. Reggie and Thurman both hit homers in Game 5, but the Yankees lost by six runs to the Dodgers. The Yankees still led the series 3-2 but if they could win the next game it would be all over; Game 6 would be tense. Dad made a series of calculated decisions, beginning with his continued support for Billy Martin and ending with both the validation of Reggie Jackson and the temporary containment of Thurman Munson's angst.

While Billy was visibly happy about the Yankees' lead in the series, Dad noticed something in Billy that he had rarely seen. Billy was insecure about his future with the Yankees. The reporters meanwhile fed his insecurity asking again and again if he would be around if he lost the series.

Billy's consequences-be-damned confidence was crumbling. Dad identified with Billy, and knew that an insecure Billy Martin meant trouble. To the reporters it was a story worth stoking, and Gabe had to move quickly and effectively to extinguish that brush fire. Dad had learned one very important lesson after the last very public battle involving Billy and Reggie: Good relationships could not trump a good story. There is always someone willing to fill in the gaps and fuel the fire. Dad was not going to repeat that mistake. It was clear that assertions that the Series would not determine Martin's future was a defunct strategy.

Just before Game 6, Dad called an impromptu press conference and he made this announcement: "We are going to keep

Billy another year, and in fact provide him with a sizable bonus. I've been thinking about it for a long time," Dad said. "I thought this was the opportune time with all the rumors and everything. I talked to George and he said do what you want. Make up your mind and just do it. You don't even have to tell me about it."

In Game 6, Reggie Jackson was benched. When the Yankees needed a pinch hitter, Billy brought Jackson to the plate. Three different pitchers delivered to Reggie's sweet spot as he topped his earlier championship performance with three back-to-back homers for the win. The Yankees had just won their first World Series in 15 years, beating the Dodgers 8-4 and giving Billy Martin, George Steinbrenner and Gabe Paul their dream come true. To top it all off, Thurman Munson gave Reggie a new nickname, "Mr. October," as Jackson was voted MVP of the 1977 Series. Howard Cosell uttered those famous words, "Ladies and gentlemen, the Bronx is burning."

New Yorkers had something wonderful and positive to talk about at a time when many say they needed it most. Dad said, "I'll never forget the ride down Broadway after the '77 Series. They said it was the biggest outpouring since the Lindbergh parade, even though it was raining. Of course winning the Series was enough, but I'll never forget the outpouring."

George was beaming and lapping up the attention that came from people outside his organization of "yes" men. "I've always kept my emotions inside me," he told *New York Times* feature writer Tony Kornheiser. "They tell me I don't let myself go. It is hard for me to enjoy myself. It is not that frequent that I really enjoy myself. It is hard to explain, but the feeling I got after winning the World Series wasn't what I thought it would be. I remember saying to myself, 'I wonder why I am not more excited?' Then I saw how happy it was making others. Then I saw that my happiness came from others being happy and them coming up and telling me. I love the little guy, the cabby, the waiter, my favorite is the one who stops me on the street and says, 'Thanks for bringing the Yankees back,'" said George.

Gabe Paul and Reggie Jackson in the Yankees clubhouse
after the 1977 World Series win

George made the rounds of the recognition dinners and speaking engagements, as did my dad, while Reggie and Billy went into retreat for a brief time. George initially gave credit where credit was due, calling Dad a brilliant man. George said, "I feel so good about winning one for New York. This is the greatest city in the world and its people are the greatest people in the world. And I just hope they like me."

On the record, Steinbrenner praised Dad, acknowledging him for putting the Yankees together and keeping relative peace among Munson, Martin and him. Off the record, George told reporters that Dad's health was deteriorating rapidly, forcing George to make the calls on the trades and the game. He left open the question of whether he would renew Dad's contract, which was due to expire on January 15, 1978. Dad took it in stride, remarking, "I'm not fearful of any consequences. It's been three months since I was offered a contract and it's just dragged on. If it bothered me, I'd do something about it."

The happy headlines about the World Series victory lasted about as long as it took the city to clean up after the ticker tape parade and the Yankee owners to count their money. As it was, the Yankees made $12 million after the 1977 World Series and paid only $150,000 to the city, thanks to a clause in the lease allowing the team to deduct maintenance fees before paying tenant taxes.

Looking for their next controversy, the writers on the sports beat congratulated Dad on the one hand for putting together a winning team, and in the next line or sound bite, suggested that Dad had bought a winner for the New York Yankees bankrolled by George Steinbrenner.

Dad did not let that pass. "That's a lot of baloney," Dad said. Well, he didn't use those words exactly when he spoke to reporters. He added, "We had a revolution; we're living with the residue of the revolution. I'd rather have the Yankees criticized for buying a pennant than for losing without getting ballplayers. Everything that is done is predicated on winning. Whether it's trading, buying or developing, you get ballplayers any way you can get them as long as it is within the rules, and this has all been within the rules. These are the rules we live by now."

"Rules we live by." That has the ring of "one rule for all," and maybe that's how Dad felt he lived his life. The season ahead brought major changes for Dad in his beloved baseball world.

Winning the World Series — fulfilling that life-long dream — set the stage for a new direction, but it seemed to be the same old silent road for the two of us.

I know Dad valued our family, but the pursuit of glory in owning a winner he made defined him, and he lived his life in pursuit of it. Seeing him there with Steinbrenner at the World Series, it looked as if Dad had chosen the Yankees and validation of his players over repairing our relationship. I never asked to speak to my dad during the Series. He had been completely unavailable to me since that game at Fenway Park in June. The World Series championship was Dad's dream, and it had come true.

I wanted to be happy about it, happy for Dad, but I just couldn't get over the fact that Dad had had so little to do with me since I let my potential career-boosting story with Reggie go. I did it for his sake, and I got nothing for it. No love, or at least no love that was evident. I was depressed, and I wanted to talk to him about it. His silence was familiar, and yet it was still uncomfortable. I made an appointment with a counselor, and I begged Dad to come. He did not believe that going to a doctor was the way you solved problems — particularly if it was emotional in nature. If you had a stiff upper lip and a strong constitution, that was acceptable to my dad. I wanted to get Dad to talk it out with the counselor and me. I wanted to believe that he valued me as much as his New York Yankees World Series championship ring. He finally agreed to come with me. Dad fell asleep in the meeting while I talked.

As much as it broke my heart, I rationalized his nap. Perhaps the continual turmoil after the victory put him off his game. Maybe he was tired from his long hours on the job. I didn't want to be angry with him, but I needed him to be there for me, and he wasn't. Dad had always said that actions spoke louder than words. In this case, his actions spoke more cruelly than I was prepared for.

My life by that time had become a discombobulated mix of ordinary and extraordinary experiences overlaid with fame and despair. I had gone through five high schools, six colleges, and a series of amazing and not-so-amazing jobs in broadcasting and sports journalism up to that point in my life. In response to my yet to be diagnosed depression I made poor life choices from obsessive shopping to choosing unavailable, needy men who drained me emotionally and financially.

I knew I needed help and I had nowhere to go. In 1978, I went into rehab at the suggestion of the counselor. I did not go because I drank too much. The counselor thought some of the programs would help me work through my questions and need to understand. We thought that maybe I could find the answer to the painful, lonely place I was at and had been careening toward since I was a child. What my dad said and did not say to me had to have an explanation, I reasoned. It had to have been hard for him, I told myself.

I agreed to enter the 30-day program because it was the only place that dealt with the sort of concerns I had. I quickly realized that the therapy focused more on combating alcoholism, and it was not for me. I was a two-drink person at most, even with Billy. Listening to the stories of the others in the program made me feel bad for them. They wanted to stop and could not. Billy and other men like him had shown me that alcohol was not an answer to pain. When it came time for me to tell my story, I was not a young girl dealing with depression. I was a celebrity and daughter of the World Series winner and team owner Gabe Paul. The counselors wanted my dad to come there. He was well enough known to cause a buzz. I asked him not to show up.

Three weeks into the program, feeling like Dad was right and I could just deal with "it" alone, I left. I was embarrassed that I tried to get help with "it." I never understood what "it" was that bothered me so and blamed myself for feeling empty.

Dear Dad,

You always remember how someone makes you feel. All parents damage their kids to some degree, but it is what people do after they are hurt that determines how history will play itself out.

You made George Steinbrenner a winner. You ran the team together, leaving just enough controversy to keep some people guessing about their futures. You knew how to rescue people, and you did it for George, Thurmon, Billy, Reggie and so many others. Why didn't you try to save me? When I was in boarding school, I took too many pills once. I thought you would come and rescue me from myself. You didn't then, and you did not come when I cried out for your help again before going to rehab at the age of 26.

You were living a dream, while mine was slipping away. In some perverse way, seeing you live out your dream validated my decision to avoid confronting you with my disappointment. I felt bad, but the reward for feeling bad was that you were happy and I protected you. It was as if I purchased your success with my sadness.

I remember you said something so cold when I asked you to come to counseling. "How much is this going to cost me?" I felt like a kid whose Dad said "No" to a raise in her weekly allowance. As ahead of my time as I was at work, I was way behind emotionally with you. When I think about how often you said actions speak louder than words and then reflect on the way we both acted toward one another, I understand why we did not connect. It was all I ever really wanted, and I did not know how to do it. My dream was never independent of my relationship with you. If we had connected and worked through it together, it would have been better for our relationship.

I miss you Dad. I love you,

Jennie

10
Afterglow

What do you do when everything you have wished and worked for actually happens? If you are Gabe Paul, the answer is easy; you do what you said you were going to do. You go back to your roots and fulfill a promise set aside during your climb to the top. Dad's long-time friend Steve O'Neill reminded him of the deal they had made when they both abandoned their attempt to buy back the Indians from Vernon Stouffer and instead bought the New York Yankees in 1973. Dad and Steve still held an affinity for the place that launched their dreams. It was said of Dad that he could "dial-a-deal" — make great trades by phone. Now Steve did his own "dial-a-deal" to remind Dad of that long deferred agreement. Dad would answer the call and leave George Steinbrenner hanging.

With a World Series championship ring on his finger and a contract not yet renewed with Steinbrenner, Dad resisted the pressure to retire at the age of 67 and rest on his accomplishments. "I've thought about retiring," he said, "but all the talk about actually doing it has been by other people, not by me. It is not my nature to retire. It may be all right for two weeks, but after that I'd go crazy, and I am not ready for the booby hatch." Dad announced his resignation from the New York Yankees effective after the Winter Baseball Meetings. He honored his contract with the Yankees to the last day.

On January 15, 1978, Gabe Paul said "Goodbye" to his stake in the New York Yankees, a team that he had helped to win two pennants and a World Series championship, ending a 15-year drought.

George Steinbrenner, himself master of the surprise attack, was beside himself at what he took as a pre-emptive strike from his president and general manager. Dad was part of George's day-to-day operations, and George knew that he could not compete with him in terms of baseball knowledge or team management expertise.

When Dad said he was leaving the Yankees, George probably figured he could get him back or at least have continued access to him just as he had in the past. But when Dad bought into another team with Steve O'Neill, George realized his control was at an end.

Dad's share of the Yankees was placed in a trust pending a sale by the trustee as required by the rules of Major League Baseball. According to author Peter Golenbock, none of the Yankee owners ever made money on their investments. My dad was the only exception. Five years after helping Steinbrenner buy into the team, Dad had to sell his shares, and Steinbrenner tried to use the owner protection clauses from the original partnership agreement, and his majority position, to force Gabe to sell those shares to him.

Steinbrenner's back channel maneuvers weren't limited to Dad. Following the Series win, others of the original ownership group left. In one example, George invited Marvin Warner, minority Yankees owner and the former U.S. Ambassador to Switzerland, to join him for dinner at an exclusive restaurant known as Le Club. When Marvin got there, he noticed that the maitre d' was wearing a New York Yankees World Series championship ring. Marvin was in good spirits as he looked toward the dining room at George, who was entertaining several others. When the head host refused to let him in, Warner looked at George, who knowingly looked back at Warner. Warner still wasn't allowed in. Marvin was indignant at this public humiliation, and he left Le Club and the New York Yankees shortly thereafter. George had first right of refusal on Marvin's stake. By 1978 owners Jess Bell, Ed Ginsberg, Sheldon Guren, Nelson Bunker Hunt, Edward Greenwald and Thomas Evans all sold to Steinbrenner in response to things he did or said, giving George 55 percent ownership of the Yankees. (The *New York Post* estimated that Steinbrenner increased his initial investment 46,000% by his death in 2010.)

With the World Series victory and two pennants, the Yankees were worth a lot more than they were when Dad, George, and the other investors bought the team from CBS. On paper, the team was worth $25 million in 1978, nearly three times the $8.8 million net cost to Dad's ownership group. George wanted to offer Dad less than fair market value for his shares. Dad flatly refused. He wanted to sell his shares to Barry Halper, a close friend. George tried to prevent Dad from selling to another based on language in the original agreement that gave him the power to block a sale to outside investors. Dad went to Bowie Kuhn to resolve the matter, but Bowie backed Steinbrenner. Dad threatened to sue, and the dispute was ultimately settled in Dad's favor. Unlike the other investors, my dad got fair value for his stock.

The fact that George could not get Dad's share annoyed him, and like a wounded animal, George fought back. "I don't mind Gabe leaving with his image intact," Steinbrenner said at spring training. "But he was in baseball for 40 years, 25 as a general manager, and did he ever win a pennant before? You think he made all those moves with this team himself? You think all of a sudden he got brilliant?"

The press corps defended Dad. One man said, "Mr. Paul had in fact put together the Cincinnati Reds pennant winners of 1961. And even if Mr. Steinbrenner was willing to take a bit of credit for the Yankees pennant winners of 1976 and World Series championships later, Mr. Paul made the trades."

Another sports reporter who knew Dad challenged George, "You called him brilliant in October."

"A brilliant baseball man, yes," responded Steinbrenner, "but he was getting old. Look, let him have his image if he wants it. I won't say anything bad about Gabe."

Hearing about the exchange, Dad smiled. "Old?! Steve O'Neill is 77, and he thinks I'm a kid. Before accepting the Cleveland job, I got medical clearance. The doctors told me I could get as physically tired as I wanted but just don't get mad. Keep your cool they told me. Aggravation kills people. If I retired, I would have deep aggravation."

Though Gabe refused to rise to the bait when reporters tried to stir up controversy, George was always good for a final word. He said, "Maybe I was too hard on him. Maybe I hurt him. If I did, I'm sorry." Who knows if he meant it?

Steinbrenner replaced Dad with two men, Cedric Tallis and Al Rosen. Then George said, "Much of the front office furor last year was a result of a communications gap between Gabe Paul and Billy Martin. I don't think we are going to see that anymore. I think Billy will get along better with the new executive vice president, Al Rosen. They played in the American League together. Billy trusts Al's judgment. Al understands Billy. I expect Rosen to get my policies across better to Billy than Gabe did. I'm not saying we won't have a disagreement here and there, but I think Billy understands the organizational policies now. He is ten times the man he was last year on this subject. With Rosen around, I'll be removing myself more from the day-to-day operation of the club. I think in a way, Gabe liked the role of being a peacekeeper last year," said Steinbrenner.

"That's horse bleep. Quote me correctly. That is horse bleep! There was no communication gap between Billy and me," said Dad. "We got along fine. I like Billy, I have always liked him, personally. I just think he needed some understanding of the total picture of the organization. I think there was no communication gap when George and Billy went at it in the Mets clubhouse in St. Petersburg last year," Dad said to reporters. "Billy was not as close as everyone thinks to being fired last year. Every manager is on the brink sometime during the course of the season. But time takes care of everything."

"When I got to the Yankees it was a nice, pleasant place to play, but as I look back, there was little pride. When a club gets that way, it ceases to function. I'm proud of the run we made in '74. I thought that was remarkable. And of course, winning two pennants and a World Series in the last two years is when all the work we did together, well, it all fell into place. I'm not surprised my contributions to the Yankees since bringing in Steinbrenner in 1973 are now being re-evaluated. There is always a minimizing effect on your production after you leave an organization. I don't want to get into a fight with George. I think everybody knows what I did there," Dad said in an interview.

Bronx Bomber fans and the media did know, and they said as much. Dick Young wrote, "Good executives are harder to replace than good athletes. New York will miss Gabe Paul as much as Tom Terrific, Clyde, Jopey, Baby, and Rod Gilbert. It just doesn't know it yet." Dad responded to the accolades with humility and optimism publicly, and he chose to keep these comments in his diary.

Looking forward to his return to Cleveland, Dad said:

Cleveland has been maligned so much and the people are so hungry for a winner, they'll look for anything that is better. It is going to be a tough go. I know what has to be done; I've been there before. It's tough to operate without money, and now I will be operating with money since Steve bought almost 60 percent of the team. He promised to put money into it. At the same time, I'll miss New York. I like New York. So does Mary. It is not easy leaving a championship club. Being a winner, your meals taste a lot better. That's what we are all in this game for, to win, and I will miss that a lot. I've had success here and that's important, but that's behind me. Reaching for something is one thing and maintaining it is something else. I believe Cleveland is a redeemable franchise. The game has been good to me, and I think I owe something to the game.

When Dad went back to the Indians, he took with him knowledge of the history of the Indians and an understanding of how to change the future. Dad went after a winning formula, first by ensuring that there was sufficient investment in the things that built winning clubs. Player development, effective trades, good management, controlling egos and making friends with the media in Cleveland were the variables he combined in his strategy. The team he returned to was fifth in its division and tenth in the league. In 1977, the Indians attendance was lower than it had been since the season after Dad and Steve O'Neill went to New York. "Cleveland is a sleeping giant," Dad said. He would attempt to awaken that giant.

I had a chance to talk about those days with Dad's long-time secretary, Barbara Lessman. She told me about her first day with him.

"He said, 'What's your name?'"

"I said, 'Barbara.'"

"Then Gabe said, 'Okay, move over there to that desk.'"

"And that's how I got the job," said Barbara. "I worked for him until he left and then for many more executives here at the Indians. I was from Pittsburgh, and my demeanor toward my new boss came more out of respect for one's elders than from my knowledge of his accomplishments. I was not well versed in the Indians or the Yankees at that time.

"After I got the job, I unpacked his things. When I hung up the picture of him with Babe Ruth, I knew I was working with a well-regarded legend. People would come to see him, and call often. Yogi Berra strolled in one day and just sat down on Gabe's couch. It is all different now. Don't get me wrong, I have some pretty incredible friendships with ballplayers now. It is just not the same as it used to be now that there are agents involved.

Gabe Paul with Babe Ruth

"When I worked for Gabe, the players used to come and talk about the game and their families. Gabe would welcome them to his office, and he would listen. He was tough, and he was hard on all his employees, including the players. He was fair, and he wanted us to do well. He was loved, hated, and truly respected. There was a really good side to him, and many people knew it — showed it," Barbara added.

December 4, 1978

Mr. Gabe Paul
Cleveland Indians Company
    Stadium
Cleveland, Ohio

Dear Gabe:

I appreciate your note congratulating me on winning the
Cy Young award. As I review the past year, I recognize
that the key to my success was having the opportunity to
pitch for the New York Yankees.

Many people may claim credit for giving me the opportunity,
but I know, more than anyone, that you played a major role
in my being the success I am today. For this I will be
eternally grateful.

Bonnie, Jamie and I, wish you the best of success in the
future and a very Merry Christmas.

Sincerely,

Ron Guidry

Ron Guidry

Note to Gabe Paul from Ron Guidry

On his return to Cleveland, Dad set communication expectations and broke old boundaries by inviting reporters to team meetings, which most major league teams, including the Yankees, forbade. Dad explained this break with tradition saying, "I don't want guys leaking anything said in an effort to get brownie points with the press. I'd rather the reporters get the information first hand." Gabe Paul wanted all his players to exhibit good character. He laid down a few ground rules including that players were not to take refuge in the training or locker rooms. A legitimate question deserved an answer. What I would not have given to have my Dad lay it out like that for me, and then follow it up.

From Dad's experience, if you took care of the press and gave them what they needed, then they would write the stories that would entice people to come to the game. Box office results would generate the revenue to help the club financially. "It's unreasonable to expect help from the press without returning the favor," Dad said. Dad gave them something to write about besides the fact that Frank Robinson was the scapegoat when he was let go as field manager for the Indians' poor performance in the 1977 season. Dad respected Frank. They went way back. When Dad was president and general manager of the Cincinnati Reds, he signed Frank, spotting his talent early on.

As an Indians owner for a second time, Dad's final years as a full-time baseball executive would be all about his ideals. If you were brave enough to argue with Gabe Paul on his baseball decisions, he would talk to you about strategy and history, demonstrating his vast knowledge and experience, respectfully. On the other hand, if you challenged him on his principles, you would see a more personal side of his character.

When Cleveland sports writer Doug Clarke was looking for a reason bigger than reality to blame for the Indian's continued poor performance, he pointed to Dad. He did not question his management tactics, but rather suggested that Dad's trading was racially prejudiced. More emotional than I had ever seen him, Dad wrote a blistering letter to the editor. In that letter to *The Cleveland Press* Editor Joe Cole, Dad pointed to his record of support for the many great black men in baseball whom he helped get where they were by treating them like everyone else. In today's world, what Dad did would be expected. At that time it was precedent setting. Dad was deeply offended by Clarke's accusation of racial bias, and he said so in the letter:

Dear Joe:

In my many years in professional baseball, I have made it a point to ignore newspaper articles regardless of their lack of authenticity. I have a reputation of not complaining. There are times when it is advisable 'not to turn the other cheek.' I find myself in that situation after reading Doug Clarke's column in yesterday's *Press* which indicated that there was racial bias and bigotry in the policy of the Cleveland Indians. Since I am the President and Chief Executive Officer of the Indians and responsible for the policy, I take personal offense to that allegation of racial bias. My record on race relations is open for close inspection and apparently completely disregarded by Mr. Clarke....

Dad's letter was printed in the newspaper. That the publication of the letter won him friends and supporters was irrelevant to Dad.

Dad received this response from *The Cleveland Press*.

Dear Mr. Paul;

Your record on race relations as well on every other subject is very clear and very outstanding, and you need apologize to no one. The article by our columnists could easily have been misinterpreted. I want you to know that I have lectured to him on the responsibilities of the press. I am sorry it happened and I certainly hope that we can make sure that it will not happen again.

Joseph E. Cole, Publisher, *The Cleveland Press*

As strongly as he objected to unfair attacks on him, Dad accepted zingers when they were true. His reaction to a "Ziggy" cartoon demonstrated this.

In Tom Wilson's syndicated cartoon, Ziggy is upset that his team, the Indians, is losing. The phone rings and the conversation bubble identifies the caller as Gabe Paul. In the comic strip,

Dad asks Ziggy for a favor. "Could you please not root for us next year?" I am not sure if Dad knew about it or not before it went to print, but his response to it was very different from his reaction to the racial accusations made by Clarke. Dad framed the Ziggy cartoon! And he smiled.

In an effort to create excitement and build a winner, Dad reminded Clevelanders who he was. With Jeff Torborg managing in place of Frank Robinson, and protégé Phil Seghi stepping back behind Dad as the assistant general manager, Dad did what he did best; he built the team with the future in mind. His decisions moved pitcher Dennis Eckersley and catcher Fred Kendall to the Red Sox for pitchers Mike Paxton, Rick Wise, third baseman Ted Cox, and catcher Bo Diaz.

"We got three potential starters and a stabilizer for our pitching staff," said Dad. "We weren't interested in one player in particular. We wanted the whole package," Dad said. "I am a man who likes to deal. I was brought up in the Branch Rickey School of never standing still with a winner. Of course, with Cleveland my choice is different. I have to reach respectability, and then go beyond it. Last year it was bankrupt. Now, we have a financially reconstructed club, and thanks to Steve O'Neill, we can buy or deal. Maybe we can get involved in a multiple player deal."

Not long after, reporters still looking for conflict questioned Dad on whether or not he made the trades for the Indians or to get back at the Yankees given the fact that he had traded Yankee pitcher Mike Torrez to Boston before switching teams himself. I can just see Dad smiling. "I've got nothing to get back at them for," he said. "That would be foolish. The only reason you make a deal is to help your club."

In addition to the Torrez trade, he brought on free agents Rich Gossage to back up Sparky Lyle, Rawly Eastwick, Jim Spencer and Andy Messersmith. When Dad left New York, the Yankees were in great shape. Each of these men would play a major role in the Yankees second World Series victory the following year, except Sparky and manager Billy Martin. The team had stayed intact after Dad left with the exception of Billy Martin, who only made it half way through the season. Losing Dad as his shield and confidant, Billy could not maintain the "everything is beautiful" attitude that he presented in spring training. When Jackson ignored Billy's orders and instead bunted into a strikeout, Billy suspended him. George Steinbrenner entered the fray, which drove Billy to provide the sound bite that sunk his career with the Yankees. Saying of Reggie and George, "They deserve each other. One's a born liar and the other is convicted," Billy sealed his fate. He was out.

By the end of the 1978 season, the Red Sox would move up a spot in the American League East and the Indians would drop a rung to sixth place, while the Yankees would take the pennant and ultimately the World Series. Dad would get the credit for the Yankees' 1978 season performance from fans and reporters. Catfish Hunter reeled in Game 6, with a little help from Rich Gossage, who didn't let any get away. Reggie brought himself and another home, ending the series with more RBIs than any player on either team. The victory in 1978 was not a surprise. I see it as a testament to the strength of a general manager when the team wins after he is gone.

When Steinbrenner's moves resulted in a significant drop in the Yankees' game results during the 1979 season, he announced that Billy Martin would be back managing the Yankees in 1980. The death of Thurman Munson had shaken the team deeply, and George struggled to deal with its effects. Injuries to Jackson and Gossage made it look like it would only get worse under current team manager Bob Lemmon, so George brought Billy back. George would fire Billy again half way through that season for punching out a marshmallow salesman. Billy moved to the Oakland Athletics.

Gabe at spring training, 1980

In 1980, Dad reflected on his decisions and the results of his actions since coming back to the Indians. The success Dad created with the Yankees would in fact hurt him later in terms of the high cost of players. Dad would never again own a team in number one position, although the rivalry with the team he helped put there would continue throughout the rest of his career. This entry from his diary dated August 18, 1980, reveals his perspective.

During the summer of 1977, I was approached by Armond Arnson about the possibility of my returning to Cleveland, with Steve O'Neill to help restore the Cleveland Club, which at that time was on the verge of bankruptcy, which probably would have meant the transfer of the franchise to another city. Later, independent of Armond's efforts, Art Modell contacted Steve O'Neill in an effort to save the franchise for Cleveland and to save a tenant for the Stadium Corp.

At any rate, Steve did come to the rescue and a very unusual financing plan was created through I.B.C. Steve was the last resort, as repeated efforts were made to interest buyers. There were none available except for Bob Short whose interest was on the basis of a very, very low price and a restructured stadium lease, which did not appeal to Modell.

Before agreeing to leave the New York Yankees and accepting the position as President and Chief Executive Officer of the Indians, I had stated my fears of great problems because of the number of partners and the past history and recommended that the way to assume ownership was to purchase assets only, start with a clean slate, and without the hangovers from the previous administrations. This presented serious bad problems to the partners, including great recovery payments. Steve, wonderful man that he is, said he was willing to suffer through the problems so as not to hurt the partners. How many people would have taken this attitude?

Before leaving the Yankees, I was offered two proposals by Steinbrenner: remain in the same capacity as President under a new contract or act as a consultant with headquarters in Tampa. I also had another very serious offer from another club as President and Chief Executive Officer.

I would not have agreed to return to Cleveland except for Steve O'Neill for whom I would go to the end of the world if asked.

When I agreed to return to Cleveland, it was with the definite understanding that I would have complete authority and that I would have the right to form or reform the organization, without exception. No organization can properly function without a strong lead. If there is divided authority and the feeling that employees can go over the head of their superior, the result can only be trouble and chaos. I am fearful this is developing.

In February 1978, when I took over, I was told, "Please don't think you can turn this around overnight. You've got to be patient because it's going to take time." I expect this same patience to be exercised by others, and I also expect the history of baseball clubs will be examined.

Many corporations have ruined baseball teams and attempted to employ their successful business methods but have failed. CBS failed miserably with the Yankees, the Wrigleys with the Cubs, Seattle with its Department Store-oriented directorship and authority, since abandoned, etc. etc. A Board of Directors cannot operate a ball club as it does a business. There cannot be divided authority or delayed decisions, as Vernon Stouffer learned in Cleveland when he tried that tactic, including hiring a high powered advertising and PR agency deferring board decisions to committee, etc.

What did I find when I took over on February 3, 1978: A bankrupt club, not wanted in Farm Club cities, divided authorities, an unsalable franchise, crooked ticket operations, possibly a number of free agents (one materialized, others were in a standoff). The organization is finally solid, rehabilitated and once again confident in general manager Phil Seghi, a good farm director in Bob Quinn, and except for one or two spots, functioning and capable.

The franchise is solid as evidenced by the requests for purchase. Only in the last week, Steve had a call. I had one from a person I know very well that Brad Corbett has expressed an interest in buying into I.B.C. There have been a number of other inquiries, which is certainly different from two and a half years ago.

In 1981, the Indians edged out the New York Yankees in the division early in the season. Everything Dad had done to that point seemed to be leading toward a winning season until the player strike interrupted the momentum. When the strike was settled, the split season method for calculating the standings knocked Dad's team below the Yankees. His former team would ultimately face Billy Martin in the American League Championship Series and sweep them. Billy Martin would be fired from the A's the following season.

Five years after he safeguarded Billy's position with the 1977 Yankees, Dad saw an opportunity to add value to the Indians by bringing Billy Martin onboard. Dad went after him for their 1983 season. When interested reporters asked why Dad wanted to hire a manager who could not seem to keep a job, Dad defended him. "Billy was on the verge of a nervous breakdown when George fired him. Sure, he is fiery, but it takes all kinds of things to make up a guy's being, and this is part of Billy. Without it, he wouldn't be the same. He might not be the manager he is. He's an excellent manager. He has a certain something that stimulates players, even ones who don't like him."

"Billy Martin sells tickets, and ticket sales mean operating capital," Dad said in explaining to the other owners the business reason that he stood behind Billy. "He gives a team confidence. Until he went to Oakland, nobody told those players anything nice. Look what he did there. He's not afraid of consequences. He's got balls. That's what good managers have: Earl Weaver, Whitey Herzog, Tommy Lasorda, Ralph Houk, Billy Martin, they've all got guts."

On behalf of the Cleveland Indians, Dad offered Billy a million dollars over three years, a far cry from the $72,000 Billy made with the Yankees. Dave Anderson of the *New York Times* said, "In any other profession Billy Martin would have been branded a loser, somebody who created more problems than he solved. But as a baseball manager, he somehow seemed exempt from that stigma. Instead of being ostracized for his tendency to self-destruct, he is glorified for his history of turning a team into a contender as soon as he took command."

George always seemed to want what Gabe had. George didn't want Billy until Gabe wanted him. Now the battle between the Indians and the Yankees was on. Gabe had already demonstrated that he would let the man manage as he saw fit, well, most of the time. Dad offered Billy money and a supportive relationship backed by knowledge and a sincere commitment to the team from majority owner Steve O'Neill. George, on the other hand, had proven that Billy would be under his thumb or out on his ass at his bidding. With both teams finishing the 1982 season in the middle of the standings, despite finishing above .500, George tried to keep Dad from signing Billy for the Indians.

Dick Young called it when he said, "they have this strange passion for each other. They can't stand each other, George Steinbrenner and Billy Martin, yet they can't stay away from each other. When one calls, the other comes running. Dr. Freud made a whole generation crazy explaining that relationship. Both take new lovers, grow quickly dissatisfied, and wind up back in each other's arms. Everybody nods, 'I told you so.'"

Billy signed with George. It had come down to money and an unhealthy choice for Billy Martin. He would be the manager for the New York Yankees in 1983 and be fired again. Billy and George would go through this back-and-forth love-hate relationship in 1985 and 1988. Billy would be there for the Yankees again but never for more than one season.

Dad understood relationships with men. That is why he was there with Steve. The two were inseparable until death. The same would be true with Billy and George. Billy was preparing to return to the Yankees as their manager in 1990 for a sixth shot at the job when he was killed in a traffic accident on Christmas.

After Steve O'Neill died, Dad stayed on long enough to ensure that his age-old promise to keep the Indians in Cleveland was fulfilled. During Gabe's second tenure with the Indians, Donald Trump offered to buy the Indians, planning to move them to New Jersey; even though Trump stated that he would keep the team in Cleveland, Dad understood his true intentions. Gabe made sure that deal did not go through by finding local buyers in the Jacobs brothers.

Dad would leave the Indians in 1984 when he finally retired at the age of 75 after 65 years in baseball. Having met his commitment to Steve O'Neill and Clevelanders, he relocated to

Tampa, Florida, the home of the only thing he loved more than baseball, my mother, Mary Frances Copps. In a curious twist, George Steinbrenner would follow him there.

October 24, 1983

Mr. Patrick O'Neill
23200 Chagrin Boulevard
Beachwood, OH 44122

Dear Pat:

This letter is to confirm our agreement made Saturday, October 22, 1983 to purchase the stock of the F.J. O'Neill Estate in the IBC Corporation prorated at thirty million dollars ($30,000,000.00).

All other stockholders in the IBC Corporation will be offered on the same basis. There will be a tender offer made to the various limited partners and the two preferred limited partners at a later date. It is my intention to keep the Cleveland Indians in Cleveland.

This agreement is subject to the finalization of documents and approval by the American League. This is all cash payable upon approval by the American League.

Sincerely,

Donald J. Trump

ACCEPTED BY:

_____
Patrick O'Neill

THE TRUMP ORGANIZATION
725 FIFTH AVENUE · NEW YORK, N. Y. 10022   212 · 832 · 2000   TELEX · 427715

Offer from Donald Trump to buy the Indians

The team Dad built did not bring home a pennant for the Indians. What Dad did was what he had done for so many other teams. He made it possible for them to win after he was gone just like he had done for the Yankees and the Reds. His secretary, Barbara, told me, "When Gabe was here with the Indians, we lost many games. Gabe never stopped believing. He worked tirelessly to build the team up again and keep us in Cleveland when that was not a very popular idea. Then in the 90s, everything changed. We moved into the new stadium in 1994, and in 1995 the Indians season erupted and the fans suddenly had the same confidence in us that Gabe Paul had when he and Steve were here. If the team was playing a game out on the West Coast, you would want to stay up late and watch them. You didn't worry about it if you fell asleep in the bottom of the ninth inning and the Indians were losing with two outs. When you woke up the next morning, you would see that they won just as you expected."

"Gabe said if the team ever made it to the World Series, everything would explode. It did. It was a magical time. It was almost as if we had to go through that much loss to get to the place where we could win. The Indians made it to the World Series that year and again in 1997 with little more than a hope and a prayer. We did not win the championship, but the pennant was good enough for us and Gabe Paul. When he was here, he fought hard for the team.

"He always tried to do the right thing, and I think he did. It was hard. There were cash calls, and keeping the team's head above water took a lot of effort. It was clear he loved baseball and he loved Steve O'Neill. Steve was a sweet man, and he took care of us all. He took care of Gabe and Gabe looked out for his elder and dear friend's legacy even after Steve passed. The Indians are in Cleveland today because of Gabe and Steve," Barbara said to me as we concluded our conversation.

My dad did so much, and yet he died like so many of us might: wondering if he said enough. I know the answer to that for him vis-à-vis me, and I believe I know what he would say if he were here today instead of in Heaven. My dad's legacy is that he simply kept his word and his principles, giving fans and owners what they wanted most — a home team that they could rally around in victory and loss. The same would be true for me and my dad many years later. First, though, it would stink like horse bleep.

By the time of the Winter Baseball Meetings when Dad announced that he would leave the Yankees and return home to Cleveland, I was again adrift. I didn't know what to do next, where to go, or how to start. I only knew I wanted to go forward to a place where the best were. I didn't know where that was, I just knew it wasn't anywhere near George or Billy or Dad. There were no dreams for me in Boston or in Cleveland. I was through letting Dad and the men he drove me to define my life. I would do what he did. I would move on.

I decided to pack my bags for St. Louis and try to get a job with the *Sporting News*, which was headquartered there. Dad had written for the publication early on in his career before Warren Giles made him his protégé so many years ago. Not only did it have a great reputation, but it was distributed nationally. I thought it would be as if I was continuing a legacy, sort of the same way as Dad and Steve O'Neill would be as owners of the Cleveland Indians again.

I was sure my credentials would get me there eventually. I finagled a transfer with TWA, which would pay my bills and still give me great opportunities to be where the stories were happening. I went to St. Louis to be away from the Yankees, to be close to but not right next to Dad, and to put some distance between me and Richard, another one of my many unhealthy relationships from my days in New York and Boston. I was optimistic about my future. I put all my energy into my next move west, and brought my emotional baggage right along with me.

Dear Dad,

I am writing to tell you that I understand you better now. More than ten years of sorting through your diary and files, combined with a lifetime of experiences, has taught me something about our father-daughter relationship and you as a man. I wanted you to teach me about your success and how you were able to give so much back to others, even when they did not support you, or worse, rejected you. I am talking about George and Billy and some of the fans and reporters in Cleveland. You gave when you did not want to. You kept your word.

You fought for what you believed in, and you stood down when it was important. You stayed in the game as long as you could and you played your best. But I think you had a lot of unresolved areas to your relationships as well. The difference is what you did with those feelings.

You lived a productive life, leaving winners behind and creating a legacy that could continue even after you were gone. Dad we are so much alike and yet somehow we did not connect when we had the chance. Like you, I am great at what I do for a living, no matter what it is, and I know what it takes to dream. We do what we need to do to restore pride and build a winner. How to sustain it is a challenge that has eluded us both in our careers, many of our relationships, and sadly with each other. I needed your presence in my life then and I miss it now.

I just wish we had more real life connection when you were alive. Instead, we chose parallel paths. Our hearts never met and we did not learn how to love each other unconditionally. I wish I had some words that I could fall back on now as I embrace my next season, Dad.

Love, Jennie

11
Final Inning

"You have to have confidence in your own judgment," I heard Dad say when the reporter questioned him on his decision to leave the New York Yankees rather than renew his contract in 1978. He had made the Bronx Bombers champions again, but he was leaving. If the media were surprised, I was dumbfounded. Who walks away from a winner, when owning that winner is all you have ever passionately dreamed about?

Dad's decision to leave the Yankees behind, and my decision to opt out of the life of the famous man's daughter in New York and Boston, were each made for all the right reasons, but did not turn out the way either of us expected and hoped. Just as Dad's move to Cleveland appeared to be the best thing that could happen for the Indians at that time, my new job in St. Louis seemed a positive step back to my passion for sports reporting. I was just getting started when suddenly I became very frightened of leading a normal life, so far away from everything that had made my life anything but normal. In the past, I had my emotional moments to be sure, but fear was new to me.

I began to question my decision to leave my volatile relationship with a Marlboro Man poser named Richard. Billy Martin was very far away, too. The long-term commitment of a mortgage was imminent but I wasn't sure that I could go through with it. I know now I was acting like a woman in the denial and bargaining stages of grief over something or someone lost. I called home to talk to Mom.

I remember telling my Mom, "I just want to give up. I thought that moving here was the right thing to do, but now I do not know what to do." I must have come across more desperate than I intended because she managed to dial the suicide prevention line while keeping me talking. Mom and I talked for hours with the suicide prevention person now a third party to our call.

I don't know exactly what I said. Whatever it was, Mom heard something in my voice that alarmed her. I was sad, but suicide was not on my mind. I just needed to talk things out and I wanted someone to listen. They did. The memory of that long conversation is overshadowed by the way I felt when the doorbell rang while I was still talking. I set the phone down to open the door. Standing there on the threshold was my Dad.

When I said I was finished and I wanted to end it all, I was talking about my attempt at conformity with the American dream, not suicide. I was thinking about skipping the closing on the house, quitting my job at TWA, and forgetting about the sports writing and broadcasting for something more free-spirited. How Mom got the message to my dad that I needed help I will never know.

Whatever she said, my dad dropped everything. He must have grabbed that always-ready-to-travel bag he kept packed and under his desk in case he needed to go somewhere to make a trade, because he was in St. Louis in a matter of hours. Dad used to say "there is a crisis everyday in baseball." On that day, I was the crisis, and he traded whatever he was planning to do to reach me instead. He was there, and I could not believe it.

It was amazing for me to see Dad there and know that he had come before my mother let me off the phone. He drove an hour from the stadium to the airport, then flew from Cleveland to St. Louis and took a cab to my apartment. Dad absolutely got credit for saving the game that day. I was shocked, happy, and grateful. Since I had not really been contemplating suicide, I did not appreciate the magnitude of his presence. All I knew was that he was there. It meant a lot to me.

The next day we did what we had to do. We went to the closing together. I got my home. We laughed. I cried. We went out to lunch. We talked. Dad wanted me to settle down, and I think that he thought his presence had in fact done that. Dad was glad that I seemed to have left Richard behind in Boston; Billy did not come up in the conversation. Dad returned to his new job in Cleveland.

Soon after Dad left, I convinced Richard, my boyfriend from Boston, the one that I had left Billy Martin for most recently, to come out to St. Louis and be with me. I had a house now, thanks to Dad's emotional support. The job at the *Sporting News* looked as if it might come through after all. Financially stable, I was looking on the sunny side of the street, as Dad said. For a period of time we all got along, and as Billy Martin used to say, "Everything was beautiful, just beautiful."

Richard and I married soon after and I became pregnant. My marriage to the Marlboro Man lasted about as long as Dad's stint in Houston all those years ago. Dad had made it clear that he felt Richard was not good enough for me. He was even less thrilled about my pregnancy. They say cats and dogs instantly know what people are like on the inside and react in kind. I guess Dads do, too. He saw what I did not. Richard denied that he was the father of our baby and he walked away. I was no stranger to men walking away, but you never get used to it.

I called Dad. I wasn't sure what I was looking for or what I expected. In the days that followed, however, we repeated our history. We said and did the things that made us love and hate each other at the same time again. When I said that Richard had left, my dad got right to the point. "Jennie, you need to get an abortion."

He said it so calmly, almost in a monotone. My reaction was anything but. I yelled words at my dad that I had never uttered before.

"How dare you talk to me like that?" I shrilled. "You have no right to tell me what to do with my body. I am not a child. You cannot control me, even though that is all you have tried to do all my life!"

I was striking out from a position of weakness, a secret pain that I had hidden from Dad. Years before I had a meaningless whirl with a chef on a cruise ship, got pregnant, and had an abortion which still haunted me. Dad's suggestion, when I was weak and scared, opened this still-raw wound. The phone was silent on his end. It gave me time to catch my breath, but not the foresight to choose my words any more carefully.

"Well guess what?!" I said even more harshly. "I know something about you, Dad. I know you are surrounded by many 'yes' men, and you like it. I'm not one of them! Don't even think you can put me in that position, again, the way you did with Reggie and Billy. I'm not one of your 'yes' people. I never will be!"

I had never laid into my dad like that. All those years when I felt so alone and unloved by a father consumed with his dream. All the times when it would have been better if someone said what no one said…it all poured out.

"Jennie, I am telling you that is what you need to do. That man won't be there for you or your child," Dad said.

"Thanks for making it perfectly clear that neither will you, Dad!" I slammed the phone into the cradle. In the silence that followed, I was consumed with sadness and guilt. Neither Dad nor I were winners that day.

Dad and I lost more than the phone connection that day. I did not call him when Richard came back to pick up his things. Richard and I had words. Something happened and things escalated fast. There was some pushing. I was on the floor. I was crying. I had a miscarriage. The baby was gone. Richard was gone. I lost them both that day. I was alone except for my sweet neighbor, Flora. I did not call Dad or Mom.

When Dad called several months later to see if I wanted to drive with him to a family event, I thought that we might talk. I had envisioned a predictable outcome based on 25 years of being his daughter as I prepared myself for a calmer conversation than the last one. I knew that Dad, like many men, many of my friend's fathers in fact, didn't do well with emotion or outbursts like our last hurtful encounter.

Dad and I never spoke about why I was no longer pregnant. We spent several hours in the car together driving from Tampa where he spent the off-season with Mom. We drove to Miami in silence through every city, stopping at more traffic lights than I can remember. Stop. Go. Stop. Just like our father-daughter relationship. Dad missed a few turns. Rather than go around the block, he just stopped in the middle of the road and backed up. It occurred to me that the way Dad drove, which was clearly by different rules than mine, was the way he got around in our relationship.

When Dad and I checked into the hotel, the first person I saw was Billy Martin. When I saw that sparkle in Billy's eyes, I felt myself falling once again into that unhealthy relationship. I still had that need to be told I was loved.

I was not surprised to see Billy. Although he wasn't invited to the family event, combining the business of baseball with family commitments was something that our family had done for years. Somehow, I thought it would be different this time, but I realized that Dad had not asked me to drive with him so we could work on our relationship. Dad met with Billy to talk about him joining the Indians in the hotel in Florida. Although I was not present for the meeting he had with Dad, my rendezvous with Billy would clarify my relationship with both men that day and so many that would follow.

When I talk about the void that Billy Martin filled for me, I am talking about the place in my heart that was available because my dad was not. I wanted my dad to love me, unconditionally to be patient and kind, to forgive all wrongs and remember only the things I did right. In truth, my relationship with my dad stopped being healthy long before I latched on to a substitute in Billy Martin.

This man was happy to be a stand-in. Billy Martin was the antithesis of a healthy relationship, not exactly what I needed, but everything that I wanted at that painful time in my life. I knew it and I welcomed Billy into my bedroom again. I told myself, if Dad was willing to take another chance on Billy Martin and the Yankees wanted him back, too, then who was I to say "No"? I could bring him back into my life and my bed. He was not marriage material, but then, considering the debacle with Richard, apparently neither was I.

Like so many men before him, Billy listened to me, told me that I was beautiful, wonderful, and good for his spirit, and that he liked me for mine. He accepted me as I was. I took that as an expression of love the way I wanted to be loved. I saw sex as returning the favor, the way a man — and definitely Billy — experienced love returned.

He looked at me the way men always looked at me instead of the loving way that I wanted. He was glad to see me, so to speak — no, it was not a souvenir baseball bat in his pocket that alerted me to this fact. Billy Martin was always ready even when he was dead drunk. That's when Billy went too far.

"Do you like my cock?"

"Give me a break! Who talks to women like that?" I said angrily, "I deserve better than that, Billy Martin!"

Billy laughed. He thought I was kidding. I pushed him away. He came toward me again.

"God!" I said, half-incredulous and half-praying at the same time.

He belched. "C'mon, Jennie," he said staggering. Was he worse than before, or had I simply had it with disrespectful dogs like Billy Martin? After a little more rejection from me, it was clear that he was not going to be able to come to the party. He left a little down, so to speak.

The next day was the family celebration. My brothers and mother were there by that time and I tried to focus on the real reason I had made this trip instead of the distraction from the previous night. I saw my brother Michael and looked at him with admiration. I was proud to be there for him that day, supporting him, honoring our relationship. I was thinking about our child-hood before and after my youngest brother Henry and I had become closer. I looked around and took in the rest of the family dynamics.

My eldest brother, Gabe Jr., had followed in Dad's footsteps on the business side of baseball when he became the Vice President of Stadium Operations for the Milwaukee Brewers and was happily married. Warren was Vice President of Kodak. I thought about Dad and Mom, their family legacy and the depth of their love for one another. Like the press, which is often on the outside looking in and trying to piece together the story, I was seeing a small slice of reality as I looked on at my family and what I saw as their fairy tale life. I guess it is the same way people on the outside thought of me.

I thought about the life my family chose, and I questioned myself. What was I doing? Why was I always playing injured? How could I love and hate my father at the same time, when all he did was love me? That is what my brothers said. From the outside looking in, everything that my brothers and mother did seemed to have put them in a place that was so much better than where I was. They had done what Dad told them to do and they seemed happy and fulfilled, unlike me. In despair, I looked at their example. I looked at Dad and Mom.

I made a big decision, a choice if you will. I decided to do it Dad's way. To say I saw the light would be more dramatic than it really was; for me it was simply about opting out of the controversial path that I had taken thus far. I buried my free spirit for a time.

I met my children's father, Bruce, soon after. He treated me with respect and was so caring at the beginning of our relationship. Dad approved of him and enjoyed talking about the Yankees with him.

Bruce Gardner, Frank Robinson, and Gabe Paul

Soon after, Bruce and I married. Dad gave us the down payment for our farm in Davidsonville, Maryland. It seemed like the right thing to do at that time. Bruce and Dad got along famously, and we had a good time together as a family when Dad would visit. Bruce opened up a restaurant and I ran a birthday party business with pony rides and appearances as a clown. We had two children, Matthew and McKenzie.

Jennie's wedding party

The intimacy between Bruce and me was not that great. I reasoned that if my dad respected him, it was enough of a positive to marry the man. Coming off of my last few less-than-loving experiences, particularly the one with Billy, I wasn't so sure that I would miss it anyway. It was not long before I knew I was wrong about missing Billy.

Three weeks after my daughter McKenzie was born on November 8, 1989, while making Thanksgiving dinner, I cut my hand in a food processor and had to be rushed to the hospital. I was bleeding profusely and had emergency surgery with over a hundred stitches and a skin graft on my left palm. The doctor ordered me to hold my left arm above my heart while I healed. With toddler Matthew and infant McKenzie, and me unable to even change diapers, there was no choice; we hired a helper. I sat a lot, watching TV, trying to heal and anxious to get back into the comforting routine of motherhood.

Christmas seemed to come quickly that year, bringing no joy with it. This holiday and my birthday have always been hard days for me as persistent reminders of my failure to build the "right" kind of life. In 1989 with a newborn, a one-year-old, and a wounded hand, I was hoping Christmas would pass without drama.

Breaking News: Billy Martin of the New York Yankees was killed today in an accident....

I never heard the rest. My mind began to play one image after another like the end of a movie where the credits are rolling, but it was pictures of Billy and me, Billy and the ballplayers, Billy and Dad, Billy and his wife, Billy and his son. BILLY, BILLY, BILLY! As tears rolled down my cheeks, I bowed my head unable to bear the weight of those images. This was Christmas. No. Not Billy. No! Not my friend, Billy. Not the one man who understood my life and let me be me. I wanted to call someone, but there was no one who knew about us, who would get what the loss meant to me.

I had never really let that relationship go, and now I had to deal with his death. Hand to my chest, I couldn't tell which was throbbing more, my shattered heart or my still-healing hand that was lower than the doctor had ordered. Why now? Why Billy? "Damn him," I thought. "He must have been drinking."

My helper didn't hear the news and I doubt she would have realized the impact if she had. I had long since put away my Yankee Princess tiara. All she knew was that I was sad and I could not take care of my newborn child due to my injury. When she saw me sobbing, she brought my beautiful baby girl to me. I looked into McKenzie's smiling eyes, and I whispered tearfully to my daughter, "I hope you never have to feel this way."

You might think that was the end for us. Billy was dead so it had to be the end, right? Well, something can only end if you let it, and I cannot. He is a ghost in my life or perhaps an angel. Every Christmas I say a prayer just for Billy:

Dear God,

I want to say a special prayer for Billy. Protect him from the hurts he endured and put him on your second base. He deserves the best. Make sure Casey is his manager. And most of all, God, let him know he was loved and is missed.

January 1990 came, and my life went on while Bruce spent most of his time at the restaurant. Dad often came to visit our family, forming the bonds with Matthew and McKenzie that I envied. I'm glad my children have wonderful memories of these days with their granddad. Although Dad's days with the Yankees, Indians, Colt .45s and Reds were long gone, his stories put us right there with him for all the jeers and cheers. He came alive when he recounted his memories, and we all enjoyed listening. Dad liked that I had a clown and party business and that in time my son and daughter joined me in performing. Dad thought the horse farm we lived on was a good place for the kids and me. I enjoyed seeing him as a grandfather, and tried to ignore that he was far more available to my kids than he was to me, even then.

Over the next years things changed gradually in my relationship with Bruce. I'm not completely sure why, but Bruce's heavy drinking, hidden up to that point, took on a more visible and dominant role in our relationship. He attended my son Matt's hockey games intoxicated, never noticing — or not caring about — the comments of people around us. We moved to separate bedrooms and then to separate lives. Bruce seemed to epitomize all the bad relationship experiences that I had had. The worst part was that he was not available to my son, my daughter, or me.

How could I have married a man who was worse than my dad had been to my brothers and me? How did a relationship choice that seemed so good at first, one that my dad had approved of, turn out so horribly wrong? Dad may not have seen it coming, but he recognized the disintegration of our marriage. He stopped coming to visit.

Gabe and Jennie Paul

The last time I saw my father, he was in a psychological slump that this baseball great did not seem to be able to pull himself out. The doctors said the fourth stroke was the reason he fell, and he was now lying so still in that hospital room with a broken hip, legs crumpled, and eyes that were gazing off in the distance, silent. It was awful to see him like this, and yet that day, we connected better than we ever had in our tumultuous father-daughter relationship.

Dad went downhill after his broken hip. He lost his ability to speak due to the TIAs and late-onset diabetes. Though his mind was still very sharp, his body was wracked with pain. Dad was there, but he was not there. Unable to come to grips with the fear and sadness that I felt at seeing him this way, I gave in to an angry heart. There was so much I had been afraid to ask all those years when I was his twenty-something daughter. There that day, I wanted answers from my dad.

> Why were you silent when your friend, Howard Cosell, put me down like that? Why didn't you stand up for me after the Nixon debacle the way you did for Billy Martin? Why didn't you teach me what you knew, as Warren Giles had done for you? Why didn't you help me to believe in myself and encourage me to follow my dreams the way you did for Frank Robinson and all the others who suffered setbacks that had little to do with their talent? Why did you let me marry the Marlboro Man look-alike and be with those men who hurt me so badly? How could you have been so indifferent to me all those years, Dad? Why couldn't you ever say you loved me?

The words were there, but they would not come out. Something got in the way of what I really wanted to say that day, just as it had all those years earlier. I wondered if the same was true for the man lying in that hospital bed. I heard him stir. I braced my-self for the way our conversations usually went. "Here it comes, the Paulisms," I muttered under my breath.

I kept quiet, waiting, hoping for a conversation that I knew would not come. I wanted him to tell me what I did not know. I waited for that familiar resounding voice.

His dry mouth opened slowly as if reaching for an extra gasp of air. His lips seemed to be working so hard, pursed, twitching, to the point where I could only stare in fear. I was holding onto his hand. By the time I caught his final word I was the one needing the doctors. The man who had worked his way to the heights of success and followed his dream with determination and skill did what had been impossible all the 47 years of my life.

He mouthed, "I love you."

I choked up with disbelief. Now, so close the end, it had finally happened. In my mind, I could almost hear Phil Rizzuto calling my dad's last at bat the way he did when Roger Maris hit his re-cord-breaking run in 1961.

"Holy cow, he did it-t-t-t-t-t-t-t!"

My eyes overflowed. I wanted to say it back to him, but my words stuck somewhere between my heart and my throat. "I love you, Dad," never came out that day. All those times I told my dad that I loved him, I never knew if he heard me. Now unable to re-spond, I hoped he could hear me at last.

I ran out of the room, down the hall, and back home to the farm in Maryland.

My dad and my second husband left me the same day. I could not afford to keep the farm on a birthday party business and the small, temporary alimony that the judge awarded in the divorce. We were forced to sell at a loss and left with debt. I missed my dad. I missed Billy Martin. With the men I loved and the place that was my business gone from my life, I lost my identity. I was no longer a wife. For a few weeks, I thought, maybe I was no longer me.

The magic was gone from my fairy tale life. Finally and reluctantly mature, I felt a hungering spirit and a sense of duty begin to overtake my sadness. At the age of 50 it was time to reinvent myself, just as I had on so many other occasions. I wanted to give the kids and me a fresh start. I picked myself up as best I could for my children's sake and moved to Nashville to work as a DJ. I knew broadcasting and I knew country music. It was not long before I had my own morning country western radio show for WYXE in Dixie, Ernie Ashworth's old radio show and the only Classic Country station in town. I played the classics because they reminded me of my childhood in the 1960s.

Jennie goes country

Back then, many celebrities came to see my dad. I remember when Dad brought one of Roger Miller's first records home, autographed, and he gave it to me. It is how I came to like country music. I nearly wore it out playing "King of the Road" in our basement and dancing with abandon. To me country music seemed so authentic, and I yearned for that sense of realism in the incredible world that I lived as the daughter of Gabe Paul.

I wanted something real. As I struggled with my grief at the loss of my dad and my marriage, I was still searching for this connection. There was a pain in the songs that I played on my show, and it matched my mood.

Off the air, my life was a single mother focused on finding a great school for my children. I wound up picking the Franklin Road Academy in Brentwood, Tennessee. The headmaster, Dr. Fred Frawley, became a friend and confidant, and said often, "Jennie, I know you are having a hard time. You will have real support in Judy Allison and Denise Jackson. You need to join their group." Judy and Bobby Allison had remarried and Denise had reunited with Alan Jackson. I was the only one of the three who remained divorced. I used to see them around all the time, but I did not have the courage to actually join their prayer group.

"You are all coping with your same pain and hurt as baseball women," said Dr. Frawley. Billy, Bruce, the Marlboro Man wannabe and all those other nameless disappointments in my life had done a number on me. What he did not know was that the Yankee without a number had done the most damage. It was yet another time in my life when I did not reach out for help when it would have been better if I did.

As tough as I was on the outside, I was really just mush on the inside. I sabotaged my relationships and myself by avoiding connections with girlfriends and peer groups, and by continuing to pick the wrong men. I thought moving to Nashville meant going back to what I had done in those magical days, when I was a twenty-something radio superstar.

I went back all right — back to what was not good for me, again and again. It would take several more years and one special night to change that once and for all.

Epilogue 2009

It was my birthday. Not one of those big ones when you think something special might happen. It was an in-between year which was appropriate since I was also in between. I was in between love and letting go of hate. I was holding on to Dad even though he had been gone for more than a decade.

I thought when Dad died that I would somehow be released from the pain of never quite measuring up. All these years later, I wanted to be gracious and understanding about our relationship, giving him credit for doing the best that he knew how. But I couldn't yet.

I was driving down the east coast from my home in Annapolis, Maryland, to take Gulfstream safety training, a necessary skill for my current career as a chef on a corporate jet. I had originally set out on my journey with the intent of visiting Mom in Tampa, but decided to delay when I learned that my former lover was there with his band, a well-known country rock band from Cincinnati. Our break-up a year before still haunted me.

As I thought more, I realized I was very much like my mother. I lost myself in every relationship I ever had. I have always depended on men in my life, often to my own detriment. I did not want to go back to that unhealthy relationship, and yet I was not over him. I settled on a lonely life without him or any man for fear that I would be seduced and then abandoned at some point.

Though I tried to be optimistic after each breakup, I was not often successful. So it was that the night before my birthday I stayed in Myrtle Beach, SC. The next day I was barely on my way when I suddenly felt very hungry. I veered down a side road off Rt. 17. A sign pointed to the Marsh Walk, a place with a nice view and a few restaurants in Murrells Inlet, just south of Myrtle Beach.

A small pub set away from where the tourists gathered, called The Whale, seemed more inviting, and that is where I met Roger crying in his beer over his dead dog, Bootsie. Roger was captain of a charter fishing boat. As I ate my sandwich and drank my root beer, Roger told me about what a faithful companion Bootsie had been. The dog had outlasted many relationships and a few off-season jobs, but now he was gone.

Billy Jenkins, Roger's first mate, apologized for his friend. "I've known Captain Roger for ten years. He is not usually like this; he is just really upset. I need to get him out of this place," Billy said.

Roger's grief over the loss of his four-legged companion was deep and painful to see. Billy clearly cared about his friend, and wanting to put him at ease, I told him not to worry. "I don't mind listening. I am not too familiar with unconditional love like that," I said in a light-hearted manner.

Billy laughed knowingly. We talked as I munched on The Whale's locally famous (with good reason) homemade potato chips.

Suddenly Roger said, "I want to go fishing! You know, my dog could crack open oyster shells that I harvested from my secret bed."

I laughed.

"No, it is true," said Billy, supporting his friend.

"Damn right, it's true. Ohhh, I miss Bootsie. He was such a good dog. Bootsie would want me to go fishing. I am going fishing," said the Captain.

"Whoa! Hey, no. Tomorrow would be a better day to take the boat out Roger," Billy said, grabbing his friend by the arm.

"I know you are right. I do not take the boat when I have had a few. Neither Bootsie, nor my wife, Carol would like that. It's just that….sniff…Bootsie and I loved to go fishing…"

Captain Roger

Realizing that I was the only one of us sober enough to drive, I said, "Hey Roger, Billy, today is my birthday. I love to go fishing. Forget the boat. There is a lot of water around here. I will drive your truck some place. Where do you want to go?"

The three of us took off in Roger's truck to his house less than a mile away. We got the gear, opting to fish off the pier and save the boat trip for another day. We settled in a spot on the dock by a tikki bar that was Billy's favorite place, The Dead Dog Saloon.

As we sat there, I realized one of the reasons that I liked fishing was my great memories of fishing with my brother Henry. Fishing has a lot in common with baseball. You put a lot into getting ready, and then you sit or stand around waiting for something to happen. We sat there and talked, waiting for a nibble. Were we a bit too loud for the people fishing there? I don't know, but I know that people nearby were interested in our conversation.

"Well," said Captain Roger, "Miss Jennie Paul, tell me about you. Where are you from? What brings you to South Carolina?" he asked, not quite leering, but looking at me the way men tended to do at this over the hill bombshell. I had grown used to it. "You can call me the Yankee Princess," I said playfully. "It's my birthday, remember? I am celebrating it with you and Billy."

"Yankees, as in New York Yankees? I am from New York originally," he said. "That was before I became a great swordfish hunter against my father's will. I have battled and beaten Mako sharks, which are bigger and more dangerous than any great white shark. That is a younger man's fight. I am married now. I am not afraid of hard work and a challenge and that is why I started my own charter fishing business. I am also a butcher at Bi Lo, but I am off tomorrow. Come back tomorrow, and I'll take you out on the boat. We will catch the biggest, best eating fish around. I'll show you where Blackbeard's boat sunk, and then I will…."

His tales went on. Tired of him doing all the talking, I blurted out something to get his attention and change the subject.

"My dad owned the Yankees. He signed Reggie Jackson, Billy Martin, Catfish Hunter and he put George Steinbrenner in the role of general partner. I know all those men. I could tell you a few stories…even one about a fish that did not get away."

Before I could say anything more, he said, "You're George Steinbrenner's daughter! Hey everyone," he said to the men nearby and a family tying up their boat to the pier, "Look over here, I'm fishing with George Steinbrenner's daughter."

"Oh brother," I thought, "not again!" I said, "This always happens. George was the front man and always got the credit for what Dad did. At the new Yankee Stadium, Steinbrenner's name is everywhere and on anything that is for sale. Billy Martin's jersey is retired and in the monument across from George's box. Although my father's name is known among the veteran players, box owners, sports reporters and staff, there is no visual recognition of my Dad anywhere in the stadium. He is the Yankee without a number. I think that is why it still hurts me every time someone says that or I see the New York Yankees logo. My dad's name ought to be embroidered on all the tags. His name and face are absent and I have grown used to that, too, but at the same time it made me mad to hear it today," I said to Roger.

To myself, I thought, "Why did it have to happen on my birthday?"

"Everyone thinks of George Steinbrenner when they hear the Yankees, but it was my dad, not George, who made the Yankees winners again with back-to-back World Series wins in 1977 and 1978. Dad got the pennant the year before that, too. Many people know Gabe Paul though. Google him, you will see what I mean! The search result will show him in almost a million references to the Yankees, the Reds, and the Indians. You won't see too much about us though," I said, regaining my composure.

"Gabe Paul, I've heard of him," said Roger. "I grew up in New York. But I felt this calling to adventure, and I went to sea on a commercial fishing boat. Hey, uh wait, are those tears? Sorry, I did not mean to make you sad on your birthday. Why are you?"

"Dad's been dead for a lot of years, Roger. People still know him, but sometimes I don't think I ever did. Hearing how much you loved your dog and then hearing Steinbrenner's name, it is hard to explain it if you did not live through it. There is a lot of pain in those memories even though I had some great times."

"Do you think they'll make it to the World Series this year?" he asked. "It's been awhile."

"Maybe, I don't know, I can't really watch them. It hurts to see how little respect they give to my Dad. His record stood for almost 20 years, before Joe Torre brought the first of three World Series victories home in 1998. It was the same year my dad died, 1998, so it sort of sticks out," I said.

Billy and Captain Roger were amazed that a woman knew so much about sports and baseball. This was the South, remember. Many women know about sports, but men still do not expect it. In many ways it is still the same as when I was a lone woman sports reporter in my twenties. I rambled on repeating many of the stories from those glory days.

"Coincidentally, Torre's winning streak had something else in common with my dad's victorious seasons. Steinbrenner was banned from baseball during both men's championship reign," I said. "After George came back, they could not pull it off again."

"I think it might happen this year, but it is early. What do you think Billy? " Roger said.

"I think I want to know more about what it was like to be the daughter of the man who owned the Yankees. I want to know what no one else knows," said the grinning first mate.

That grin...just like Billy Martin. I knew what he meant. I told my story to the two fishermen and the others who were listening in nearby.

"I dated Billy." I said it like it was nothing. The chatter stopped. The only thing you could hear was a gentle wake hitting the pilings.

Billy, Roger's first mate, popped open a beer can. He held his hands up, shaking his head. "I wish," he said.

"I meant Billy Martin," I said smiling. "The Dead Dog Saloon over there made me think of that just now. He was a bit of a hot-dog. Who knows, maybe he is playing second base for the angels and Dad owns the team. Maybe they're winning," I said, trying to keep the conversation light. Billy Jenkins' eyes were on me the same way Martin's were long ago. There was something about Roger's first mate that reminded me of my Yankee lover. The onlookers were not shy about listening in and I did not mind it.

Some of the people listening were baseball fans. One even sported a New York Yankees hat — she was about seven and holding tightly to her daddy's hand. As much as they wanted to know about Dad, they also wanted to know about our relationship.

They sat fascinated as I recounted Dad's days as President of the New York Yankees when they were in desperate need of a championship. "It was a time," I said, "when the Mantles and Marises had long since left the city that never sleeps...." I found myself repeating words that I had spoken at a baseball history conference and at the Naval Academy when they asked me to speak about Dad and me earlier that year.

And just as on those occasions, there were the heartfelt questions. "How can a Dad...ahem.... How can I make sure my daughter knows that I love her, that I wanted to say the right thing and be there for her, even when I was not?" the stranger said with a bewildered look.

I had their attention, which wasn't bad. Actually, I loved that part. I hated reliving my pain from my Yankee years, but it was something that I was already doing day in and day out. They listened, and then some wanted to tell their own father-daughter stories. I started to realize that Dad and I were not the only ones to misunderstand one another's expressions of love. It was validating on the one hand that I was not alone in my experiences and feelings. At the same time, knowing their pain, I was sad for them. I wanted to say, "Just tell her...just stand up for her...just...."

"Oh. Oh. I've got a bite!" I yanked the line and pulled up a fish. It landed on the dock with a slap. A somewhat tipsy Roger stepped unsteadily toward my fishing pole, which I had let go of in my excitement. The fish was flopping around, forcing the small group of curious listeners to step back. The heavy emotion on the dock broke as Billy grabbed the net and scooped up my catch. Roger grabbed the rod, telling me about the time that his friend lost his expensive pole and how he had saved it, although it was nothing compared to the lives he saved in his younger days.

As Roger warmed to his sea stories, I thought about the synchronicity of the people surrounding me on my birthday so many years after Dad died. The irony of catching a fish next to the Dead Dog Saloon was not lost on me. "It would have been perfect had it been a catfish," I thought. But it was only a flounder. I laughed realizing that this fish was a lot closer to where I was in my life now that I was in my late 50s.

"That is a big fish, Jennie! We can clean it and fry up this fish for dinner at Roger and Carol's house," said Billy.

"Okay, I'll drive," I said to Roger and Billy.

Roger, smiled, nodding to Billy and me. "My wife is the best woman you will ever meet." When we got back to his house, Captain Roger said, "Hey honey, meet Jennie. She caught this fish. Long before that, her Dad owned the New York Yankees! And he loved her." A friend of theirs visiting from Boston exclaimed, "Your Dad is George Steinbrenner!"

That lovely afternoon with my new friends, our conversation became quiet and personal. That is when I told them about Dad's diary. I told the Captain that I had searched the files, looking for a letter or a message from Dad so I would know that he loved me as much as he loved making, owning, and running winning baseball teams. I was crying when I told the Captain that I did not find the answer or the words that I had been looking for from my dad.

"Are you sure about that Jennie? Wisdom proves itself to be right by what it does." That wise captain, said, drying my tears, and giving me a hug.

I laughed and winked at the captain. What he said had just sunk in. Billy smiled.

"I like the Yankees," said Carol, Roger's wife.

"I hate the Yankees," said the woman from Boston.

I was warmed by our last hours together, but the sun was going down and I knew it was time to be on my way. First mate Billy walked me back to my car. The wind picked up and I pulled my sweater closer around me, wondering how I was going to say goodbye to my birthday man, a sort of stand-in for Billy Martin, who like so many men would soon be gone from my life. I unlocked the door and turned to him, not sure what words would come out of my mouth. I didn't have to say anything. Looking like he could not let me or my smile go just yet, Billy kissed my lips. I tasted his tongue, and pulled away. "Wonderful," he said. There was a sparkle in his eye that reminded me of Billy Martin because I wanted it to. Billy Jenkins closed my car door and I drove away.

Back on Rt. 17, I continued down the road. I had to be in Georgia that night. But twenty minutes further along the dark two-lane road, I drove by a restaurant that seemed to appear out of nowhere there on Pawley's Island. I caught the sparkling lights out of the corner of my eye and made a U-turn to see why so many cars had gathered there. The sign said Frank's but I was drawn to a lighted path that led to an area behind the restaurant. There was a raging fire, outdoor heaters, a fish pond, and people joyously talking in a tented bar that was like something from a movie. I was hungry again and a glass of wine also seemed very appealing.

"Hi, I'm Flo!" said the woman next to me at the bar. I was taken aback by her friendliness at first. I had been fishing all day, and I looked like it. Flo didn't seem to mind. She was so welcoming and genuine that I relaxed very quickly. I learned that she was passionate about her job as an elementary school teacher at the Low Country Prep School in Pawley's Island. Miss Flo shared that she was a single mother with two grown children, Rivers and Kari. She had many friends including John and Sheila Besser, a nice couple who bought me dinner on my birthday.

Flo told me that her daddy had developed much of the island and Litchfield Beach many years ago, and that she, like so many others in the community, loved him still even though he was gone. Flo said that she had a wonderful relationship with her dad. It was a perfect segue to this seemingly insatiable need that I had on this day in particular to talk about my dad. There were Yankees fans there and people that loved the Indians and Reds, too. I shared how I felt about my dad and that I was celebrating my birthday, alone. Flo and I were two daughters sharing stories about our fathers. When I said that my dad died before I could fully appreciate how much he meant to me and that I did not know about all the times that he stood up for me, she was sympathetic. It felt good to talk it out. It was a perfect ending to a great day, I thought. Little did I know, God was not finished with me yet.

Walking out to my car, I stopped and looked up. The majestic Pawley's Island sky was filled with a bright moon and thousands of stars, more stars than I had seen with any of the Billies in my life. The moon illuminated a few clouds creating a surreal scene. I noticed one cloud that looked like a donut; maybe it only looked like a donut to me. Dad was on my mind all day, and the donut-shaped cloud reminded me of one of Dad's most frequently-used Paulisms: "Jennie, don't look at the hole in the donut. Look at the whole donut," Dad used to say.

I decided that maybe it was time to stop thinking so much about my "daddy hole." I resolved once and for all to look at my whole daddy and to stop blaming him. After people are dead, they can no longer love, hate, or envy. They can no longer share what happens here on Earth. I am still alive.

While I could not change the fact that Dad did not say what I needed to hear, I resolved to try to make healthier choices personally and encourage fathers and daughters to recognize each other's strengths and weaknesses, and to love one another openly and unconditionally while they are both living. I started thinking that maybe the insight on why and how Dad and I lost so many balls in the sun after he bought the New York Yankees and later when he returned to the Indians could be a great starting point for a conversation for fathers and daughters everywhere. As I've said, a woman often goes her whole life looking for her father, which is sad, because usually he is just a phone call away.

I felt that my dad was with me on my 58th birthday. He was in some ways larger than life itself, which is probably why they still talk and write about him more than ten years after he died. Dad meant everything to me, and he was more important to baseball than many sporting a New York Yankees cap will ever know. I heard myself say aloud, "It would have been better if only someone had said what no one had said."

And that's when it started to happen. My lips came together slowly, awkwardly, forming words that had not rolled off them for too long.

"I Love You, Dad. I realize, now that I am your legacy and that you were far more than the Cincinnati Reds, Houston Colt .45s Cleveland Indians, and New York Yankees personified." A great peace came over me, and that is when I knew stopping at The Whale for lunch and Frank's Outback for dinner was more than a healthy choice. Before I stopped in Murrells Inlet and Pawley's Island in South Carolina, I was stuck somewhere in between a lot of things — healing, reeling, forgiving, loving, hating. When I left, I was finally on my way to the first day of the rest of my life. It was a great birthday present.

I am Jennie Paul, and I was once a Yankee Princess.
Correction.
I am Jennie Paul, and I am *still* The Yankee Princess.

Epilogue 2010

My experience in South Carolina set me on a better path, yet as much as I tried to let go of my misunderstanding of my father, there was a gnawing question that surfaced at the most unexpected times. I wanted to know why he was the way he was. In writing this book, I resolved my "daddy hole," but to say I understood it totally would be understating the complexity. There was still a missing piece, a piece that had been hidden from me. Just recently, I have learned something about the influence of growing up Jewish must have had on Dad.

I never knew my grandparents on my father's side, but I knew that Morris and Celia Paul came from the Ukraine area of Russia. Celia died after being hit by a truck while taking a cake to a sick lady across the street, and not long after that my grandfather died of a broken heart. I loved that story because it told me how deeply Morris loved my grandmother, though I don't believe he showed his emotions to others. A tailor by trade, my grandfather was true to the culture of his parents and their life in Russia.

The cultural lifestyles in one's past are passed down from generation to generation. Feelings aside, in Russia small Jewish children learned early on to remain tight-lipped and to stay off the radar. They learned trades and that a good work ethic was respected, but to call attention to themselves would have been seen as a weakness and dangerous. They were living in a place and time where Jews were the targets of vicious and deadly pogroms — those periodic mob killings that today we would call genocide. You learned to keep your opinions to yourself and to not draw attention.

Although my father could never verbalize his cultural up-bringing, and I never saw him walk into a temple, I knew he had a strong faith. There were 12 kids in his family, all born in the U.S., and he considered himself an American with a large family. But the cultural rules of his family's history influenced him deeply, and all but two of his siblings — one brother and one sister — showed the same effects. They were silent when it came to their feelings, even with those closest to them.

I think now I understand that part of my father a little better. It doesn't answer everything, but it helps, and I am that much closer to seeing the complete picture of that brilliant and complex man I called Dad.

Appendix A

Gabe Paul Timeline

Gabe Paul's baseball career spanned more than 60 years.

1920	Bat boy, Rochester Red Wings (age 10)
1926 - 1936	Publicity Director/Ticket Manager/Traveling Secretary, "AAA" Rochester Red Wings
1936 - 1950	Assistant to the Vice President, Baseball Operations, Cincinnati Reds
1951 - 1960	President, General Manager, owner, Cincinnati Reds
1961	General Manager, Houston Colt .45s
1962 -1973	President, General Manager, part owner Cleveland Indians
1973 -1977	President, General Manager, part owner, New York Yankees
1978 - 1984	President, part owner, Cleveland Indians

Gabe's "Paulisms"

Gabe Paul had stock answers that fit any situation without actually saying anything. He used them on ball players, press, and our family. To which I would always respond, "Dad, you treat me just like a ball player. I am *not* one of your rookie ball players!

"Look on the sunny side of the street."

"Don't look at the hole in the donut; look at the whole donut."

"One man's ice cream is another man's shit."

"You are judged by the company you keep."

"There is a law of percentages."

"It will stop raining. It always does."

"If two people agree on everything, one person is unnecessary."

"Watch out for free advice. It's worth what you pay for it."

Appendix B
Additional photos and documents

About ninteen hundred and twenty nine
There was fuzz on the face of a friend of mine.

It wasn't becoming to that handsome lad
And in his position it looked xxxxxxxx very bad.

So one morning in June, the boss called him in
And gave him a razor to use on his chin.

Now that boy has a son who is just fourteen
And on his face some fuzz can be seen

So *I'm* giving the first razor to his first son
Expressinggg confidence in things to come.

It's a mark of distiction to shave the first time
For kids childish ways—it's the end of the line.

The ben's now a man and to be treated that way
But only as long as a young man he'll stay.

So before the hair on your face, gets too thick
I'll present you with this beautiful Schick.

*Given to me with my first
razor by Warren Giles in 1929*

Note from Warren Giles to Gabe with the gift of his first razor.

Note to Gabe from Branch Rickey

Michael and Jennie Paul

Michael is wearing a T-shirt from the Cuban baseball team the Havana Sugar Kings. The team was owned by Dad's friend Bobby Maduro whom he met on trips to Cuba to scout players. I remember Mom and Dad going to Cuba before anyone else and bringing us back sugar cane. Castro was a huge baseball fan and took the Sugar Kings team away from Bobby, forcing him to escape with his family.

Bobby's wife, Fufala, always asked how Mom did it with only one housekeeper when she had one nanny per kid. Her lifestyle changed dramatically when they came to the US. Once a wealthy man with seven maids for seven kids, Bobby arrived in Miami with one dollar in his pocket. Dad helped him get back on his feet.

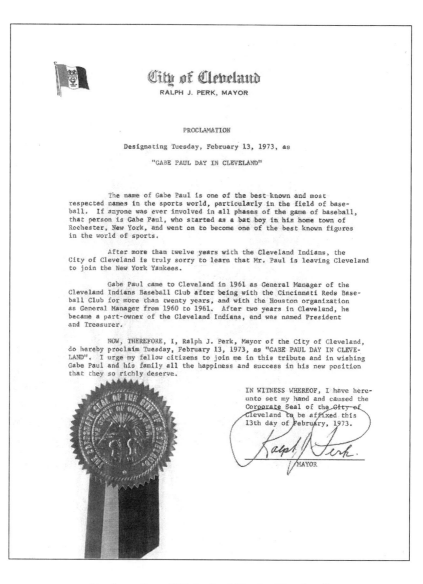

City of Cleveland
RALPH J. PERK, MAYOR

PROCLAMATION

Designating Tuesday, February 13, 1973, as

"GABE PAUL DAY IN CLEVELAND"

The name of Gabe Paul is one of the best known and most respected names in the sports world, particularly in the field of baseball. If anyone was ever involved in all phases of the game of baseball, that person is Gabe Paul, who started as a bat boy in his home town of Rochester, New York, and went on to become one of the best known figures in the world of sports.

After more than twelve years with the Cleveland Indians, the City of Cleveland is truly sorry to learn that Mr. Paul is leaving Cleveland to join the New York Yankees.

Gabe Paul came to Cleveland in 1961 as General Manager of the Cleveland Indians Baseball Club after being with the Cincinnati Reds Baseball Club for more than twenty years, and with the Houston organization as General Manager from 1960 to 1961. After two years in Cleveland, he became a part-owner of the Cleveland Indians, and was named President and Treasurer.

NOW, THEREFORE, I, Ralph J. Perk, Mayor of the City of Cleveland, do hereby proclaim Tuesday, February 13, 1973, as "GABE PAUL DAY IN CLEVELAND". I urge my fellow citizens to join me in this tribute and in wishing Gabe Paul and his family all the happiness and success in his new position that they so richly deserve.

IN WITNESS WHEREOF, I have hereunto set my hand and caused the Corporate Seal of the City of Cleveland to be affixed this 13th day of February, 1973.

Ralph J. Perk.
MAYOR

Proclamation of "Gabe Paul Day in Cleveland"
February 13, 1973

Undated note in Gabe Paul's handwriting noting that George Steinbrenner
ordered the revision of minutes of a meeting

"GMS had this gone over and amended to his convenience, such as he didn't think we would draw 1,350,000 as budgeted but acceded to these in the organization. What a hedge and what a lot of crap.

There were other alterations in the minutes.

We are back to the Stouffer committee system."

New York Yankees

GABRIEL PAUL
PRESIDENT

PARKS ADMINISTRATION BUILDING
FLUSHING, NEW YORK 11368
(212) 592-8200

Dear Bowie:

On March 20th, I called you and reached you while you were having lunch at the Valencia in Tampa. I explained my financial situation and requested permission to go directly to Mr. George Steinbrenner, for a club loan to pay my latest Partners call, because, as I explained, that with the background, etc., I felt that this was the only way to handle this situation. You agreed and said for me to go ahead but to send you a copy of the memo that I wrote to Mr. Steinbrenner.

I complied with your request and complied with everything that you requested me to do. Suddenly, two or three days later, after the memo had been sent and the matter had been put in motion, I received a call from Sandy Hadden and he said that he had been thinking about this thing and that he had second thoughts. Then I received your letter of April 2nd, in which you did a ninety degree flip, reneged on your permission and created considerable embarrassment to me. Your lack of consideration to someone who has been in the game for almost fifty years in appalling. Your failure to keep your word is equally appalling.

Please don't be concerned about your image so much that the well being of others is hurt. You made a federal case out of a very simple request. I must say that you are still so busy looking at the flea circus that you are missing the elephants.

Then I learned the other day of another involvment which indicates that you do have a double set of standards.

Letter to Bowie Kuhn from Gabe Paul — page 1 of 2

We have worked hard and the Partners have invested great amounts of money to re-establish the Yankees. The road-blocks you have put in the Club's path, and your lack of consideration and realism in my case, makes it difficult to maintain our position and operate on a proper basis.

Very truly yours,

Mr. Bowie Kuhn
Baseball Commissioner
15 West 51st Street
New York, New York 10019

April 7th, 1975/d

cc: Pat Cunningham

Letter to Bowie Kuhn from Gabe Paul — page 2 of 2

Gabe Paul, Steve O'Neill, Billy Martin

New York Yankees

Office Communication

to: BILLY MARTIN

from: GABE PAUL

May 23, 1977

I realize that you were emotional and upset after the game Saturday, May 21st, but part of a manager's job is to meet with the Press at certain times. One of the traditional times is after a game.

Making yourself unavailable in an "off limit" room is not the answer. Meeting with the Press after a game is company policy and is in the best interests of the Yankees. You must adhere to these policies and represent the Yankees under the terms of your contract, which in this case you did not do.

Needless to say I am also sure that you are aware that your actions in "shoving" a writer are not in the best interests of the Yankees either.

Gabe Paul

Memo to Billy Martin from Gabe Paul

Warren Paul, Jennie Paul, Henry Paul, and Michael Paul

Nancy Giles, Bill Giles, Jennie Paul, Henry Paul, Rosella Paul

Jennie Paul with George Steinbrenner at the first game of the NHL Tampa Bay Lightning in 1992. The expansion team was owned by Jennie's younger brother Henry Paul and Phil Esposito.

Gabe Paul with Tommy Lasorda

'RO TUESDAY, APRIL 28, 1998   L   B7

OBITUARIES

The New York Times

Gabe Paul speaking at a news conference in 1973 after the Yankees were sold to a group headed by George Steinbrenner, left. At right is Michael Burke, who had run the team before CBS put it up for sale.

Gabe Paul, Ex-Yankee Official, Dies at 88

By RICHARD GOLDSTEIN

Gabe Paul, the baseball executive who arranged for George Steinbrenner to buy the Yankees, then built their championship teams of the late 1970's, died on Sunday at Memorial Hospital of Tampa (Fla.). Mr. Paul, who lived in Tampa, was 88.

He started out as a minor league batboy in 1920, he was still going strong as president of the Cleveland Indians in the 1980's, and in between, Mr. Paul bought, sold and traded more than 500 players.

David LeFevre, a lawyer who once tried to buy the Indians, remarked, "I want to stand next to Gabe Paul when they drop the atomic bomb."

What he meant, said the Cleveland sportscaster Pete Franklin, was that "Gabe was the ultimate baseball survivor."

"He was very intelligent, a great self-promoter, and a guy who knew how to get next to people with money," Mr. Franklin once observed.

Mr. Paul survived for only five years with the Yankees, but he engineered a host of shrewd deals and spent Mr. Steinbrenner's money freely at the dawn of free agency.

After Mr. Paul left the Yankees in January 1978 for a second stint with the Indians, Mr. Steinbrenner remarked: "He was in baseball for 40 years, and did he ever win a pennant before? You think he made all those brilliant moves with this team himself? You think all of a sudden he got brilliant?"

Mr. Paul had, in fact, put together the Cincinnati Reds' pennant winners of 1961. And even if Mr. Steinbrenner was willing to take a bit of credit for the Yankees' pennant winners of 1976 and 1978, Mr. Paul made the trades that brought Willie Randolph, Chris Chambliss, Bucky Dent, Lou Piniella, Mickey Rivers and Ed Figueroa (along with Graig Nettles, whom Mr. Paul dealt to New York shortly before he arrived there from the Indians). Mr. Paul, meanwhile, signed some of the first free-agent stars, getting Jim (Catfish) Hunter, Reggie Jackson and Don Gullett. When he was not dealing, Mr. Paul served as a buffer between Mr. Steinbrenner and Manager Billy Martin.

Gabriel Howard Paul was born in Rochester, the son of a tailor. At age 10, he was the batboy for his hometown Red Wings of the International League and was conspiring with their manager, George Stallings, who had run the Miracle Braves of 1914, to give the home team an edge. When the Red Wings led in the late innings, Stallings dispatched young Paul to a grocery store behind left field where baseballs were stored in an ice box. The balls, deadened by the cold, would be slipped into the umpire's supply for the visitors' final at-bats.

Mr. Paul got his big break in 1928, when he was earning $1.50 a week as a part-time sportswriter. Warren Giles, the newly named president of the Red Wings, hired him at $60 a month to accompany the team to its Louisiana spring training site and file stories for Rochester's papers.

"I took the job for six weeks and was with him for 23 years," Mr. Paul would note.

Mr. Giles soon gave Mr. Paul various full-time front-office jobs, and in November 1936, when Mr. Giles became general manager of the Cincinnati Reds, he took Mr. Paul along as publicity director. Mr. Paul became the Reds' general manager in September 1951 after Mr. Giles was named National League president.

A lifelong baseball man who pointed George Steinbrenner toward New York.

In 1957, Mr. Paul engineered a stunt far more spectacular than the frozen-baseballs scheme. Back then, the fans voted for members of the All-Star team by checking names on ballots printed in newspapers. Mr. Paul arranged for the two Cincinnati papers to print the Reds' starting lineup every day in a sample ballot and indicate where fans could mark their "X." He had similar ballots distributed at the Reds' Crosley Field. The Reds would finish fourth that year, but when the ballots were tallied for the midsummer game, seven players from the Cincinnati lineup — infielders Johnny Temple, Roy McMillan and Don Hoak, outfielders Frank Robinson, Gus Bell and Wally Post, and catcher Ed Bailey — had been voted as the starting National League All-Stars.

Commissioner Ford Frick removed Bell and Post, replacing them with a couple of runners-up named Mays and Aaron. The next season, baseball took the vote away from the fans — giving it to the players — and did not change back until 1970.

Mr. Paul stayed with the Reds through 1960, building the team that won the N.L. pennant the next year, then worked briefly for the expansion Houston franchise before joining the Indians as general manager.

Mr. Paul became friends with Mr. Steinbrenner, who was based in Cleveland as chairman of the American Shipbuilding Company. When the Columbia Broadcasting System decided to sell the Yankees, Mr. Paul put Mr. Steinbrenner in touch with Michael Burke, who was running the team, and in January 1973, Mr. Steinbrenner and a group of limited partners bought the club for $10 million. Mr. Paul was then brought to New York by Mr. Steinbrenner as a limited partner, and he eventually became the club president.

Mr. Paul stayed with the Yankees until the beginning of 1978, returning to Cleveland to run the Indians for Steve O'Neill, his longtime friend, who had also been a limited partner with the Yankees. Mr. Paul remained in Cleveland until he retired after the 1984 season.

The Yankees observed a moment of silence for Mr. Paul before last night's game with Toronto at Yankee Stadium. Mr. Steinbrenner issued a statement calling Mr. Paul "a dear friend and the most knowledgeable baseball man I ever met."

Mr. Paul is survived by his wife, Mary; four sons, Gabriel Jr., of Reston, Va.; Warren, of Plano, Tex; Michael, of Boca Raton, Fla., and Henry, of Tampa; a daughter, Jennie Gardner, of Gambrills, Md; a brother, Sam, of Woodmere, N.Y.; three sisters, Bess Benewick, of Rochester; Mildred Levine, of Oneonta, N.Y., and Sylvia Lasky, of Olean, N.Y.; and nine grandchildren.

Of all his deals, Mr. Paul was particularly pleased with the time he got the best of that master trader Branch Rickey, obtaining the slugging outfielder Gus Bell for the Reds from Mr. Rickey's Pittsburgh Pirates before the 1953 season.

As Mr. Paul told it: "Rickey didn't like Gus's wife. He thought she was extravagant. He once told me, 'She throws diapers away.' After we finally put the deal together, Gus and his wife came to Cincinnati for the announcement, and his wife had a baby in her arms. I remember she had to change the baby's diaper, and she put him on a blanket on a table in my office. 'These are something new,' she said. 'Disposable diapers.' If only Rickey had known."

That baby was Buddy Bell, who in 1978 played third base for the Indians. When the season ended, Gabe Paul traded him.

More obituaries appear on the next page.

Gabe Paul obituary, April 28, 1998

DENNIS J. KUCINICH
10TH DISTRICT, OHIO

1730 LONGWORTH OFFICE BUILDING
WASHINGTON, D.C. 20515
(202) 225-5871

14400 DETROIT AVENUE
LAKEWOOD, OHIO 44107
(216) 228-8850

Congress of the United States
House of Representatives

Committees:
Government Oversight

Education
and the
Workforce

May 21, 1998

Ms. Mary Frances Paul
5115 South Nichol Street
Crescent Place
Tampa, Florida 33611

Dear Ms. Paul:

On February 24, 1998, I stood before my colleagues in the U.S. House of Representatives to recognize your late husband's important legacy in Cleveland baseball history. Enclosed is a copy of my remarks as printed into the Congressional Record

Due in large part to his vision in the lean years between 1961 and 1974, the Cleveland Indians remain a treasured part of the community, playing before sell out crowds each and every game. Thousands of Clevelanders have grown up with the Indians through all of their triumphs and failures. Gabe's unyielding faith in Cleveland as a baseball town ensured that this tradition will continue for many generations to come.

Allow me to extend my condolences for your loss.

Sincerely,

Dennis J. Kucinich
Member of Congress

DJK:ina

Letter to Mary Paul from Rep. Dennis Kucinich

Daughter of baseball magnate pens her tale from Clay Street

Local author's father is Gabe Paul, Yankees' former president

By NICOLE YOUNG
Staff Writer

Jennie Paul's father always told her not to look at the hole in the doughnut, but rather look at the whole doughnut — the same sentiment he shared with the 1977 world champion New York Yankees.

It is with those big-picture eyes that Ms. Paul, 56, views her Clay Street neighborhood where she's writing "Yankee Princess," a book about her relationship with her father, Gabe Paul, the president of the Yankees who worked under owner George Steinbrenner.

Two and a half years ago, when she moved into her row home in the 200 block of Clay Street, she heard gunshots fired the very first night.

Tucked away just around the corner from Annapolis's historic and tourist-driven downtown is Clay Street — home of two public housing communities. It's known for open-air drug markets

"I have no fear on this street. If you let your fears get the better of you, you'll never live."

— Jennie Paul,
whose book in progress is titled "Yankee Princess"

and other often-violent crimes, including a recent murder and numerous shootings.

Since she moved in, Ms. Paul has found that some pizza delivery places won't even deliver to her street. But the most shocking revelation came when the parents of some of her daughter's friends wouldn't let them come over to visit.

"I have no fear on this street," Ms. Paul said. "If you let your fears get the better of you, you'll never live. Either you have guts or you don't. It's in your

(See PAUL, Page A6)

By Nicole Young — The Capital
Jennie Paul displays a baseball with the image of her father, Gabe Paul, president of the 1977 New York Yankees, World Series champs. She has been working on a book about her relationship with her father and baseball from her home on Clay Street.

Capital-Gazette (Annapolis, MD) September 4, 2007

McKenzie Gardner, Mary Paul, Matthew Gardner, Jennie Paul

About the Authors

Jennie Paul

Jennie Paul is the only daughter of Baseball Hall of Fame nominee and former New York Yankees owner and President, Gabe Paul. She was an active member and observer of the tumultuous New York Yankees era of the 1970's known as "The Bronx Zoo," giving her unique access and inside knowledge for this book.

Starting her career at age 19, Jennie was a sportswriter and on-air sportscaster for WNEW-TV Channel 5 in New York City while Gabe owned and ran the Yankees. She also worked for *The Washington Post* sports editor Shirley Povich, and for the Pulitzer Prize-winning *Dayton Daily News* as a sports columnist and beat reporter covering baseball, football, hockey, tennis, and bowling. She reported on-air feature stories for "Sports Extra" on WNEW TV-5 in New York City.

Jennie became the first woman in the country to do a sports trivia radio show on the Boston Red Sox station, WITS. She covered the Cincinnati Reds, the Bengals, the Kentucky Derby, and the Indianapolis 500 for WCPO TV-9 and WLW-TV in Cincinnati. She headed to New York as Assistant Editor of Features for CBS's "The NFL Today" with Brent Musburger, Irv Cross, and Phyllis George. Following that, Jennie went back on the air for NBC Sports "GrandStand" with Bryant Gumble and wrote for the *Sporting News*, the "Bible of baseball."

Jennie Paul resides in Annapolis, MD with her two children, college students Matthew and McKenzie Gardner.

Jody Lynn Smith

Jody Lynn Smith is the author of *Talk a Different Game at Work*. Her 25-year career in public relations includes writing for small businesses, Fortune 500 companies, the Federal government, and non-profit organizations.

Smith holds a BA in Communications from Penn State and an MBA from Southern New Hampshire University. She is the recipient of many awards including the Tribute to Women in Industry award. Jody Lynn Smith lives in Myrtle Beach with her son.

Index

D

E

F

G

H

CPSIA information can be obtained at www.ICGtesting.com
227464LV00005B/19/P